D1616238

COOKING WITH
COLETTE

COOKING WITH COLETTE

by Colette Rossant,
edited by Lorraine Davis

ILLUSTRATIONS BY JAMES ROSSANT

CHARLES SCRIBNER'S SONS, NEW YORK

PARENTS' ALERT

The recipes in this book are simple but special; some of the ingredients may be new to you or to your child. You may want to check anything unfamiliar before cooking and taste carefully as you go along.

Some of the recipes include brandy, wine, or other alcoholic beverages used as flavorings. When the dish is cooked, the alcohol evaporates and only the flavor remains. These ingredients function in the same way as vanilla extract—which also contains alcohol and is used in the same way.

Be sure to give your child basic instructions on safety in the kitchen: how to use knives, stoves, potholders; how to light matches for ovens and flambé dishes. You might also want to give your child some general rules about how to deal with such kitchen emergencies as fires and cuts; and, of course, young children should never be allowed to cook alone.

While each family has its own standards of hygiene, a review of hand washing, care of fingernails, and the question of sharing "tastes" might be discussed.

Anyone who cooks should be careful about tying hair back, since the slightest contact with an open flame could be dangerous. Long hair must always be worn in a ponytail in the kitchen.

With these basics from you, your child can have a wonderful time cooking with Colette.

Text copyright © 1975 Colette Rossant and Lorraine Davis
Illustrations copyright © 1975 James Rossant

Library of Congress Cataloging in Publication Data

Rossant, Colette.
  Cooking with Colette.

  Includes index.
  SUMMARY: A step-by-step method of learning to cook
for all ages. Includes how to buy the ingredients, how
to get them ready for cooking, and how to prepare the
dish.
  1. Cookery. [1. Cookery] I. Davis, Lorraine,
joint author. II. Rossant, James. III. Title.
TX652.R672   641.5   75-16113
ISBN 0-684-14267-8

1 3 5 7 9 11 13 15 17 19 C/C 20 18 16 14 12 10 8 6 4 2

Printed in the United States of America

To Jim, Marianne, Juliette, Cécile, Thomas,
and my friend Alan

CONTENTS

Have you taken a bubble bath and played with the bubbles?

INTRODUCTION

Colette Rossant is not very tall; she has springy penny-colored curls, a lilty voice (she's half French), and flashy dark eyes (she's half Egyptian). A teacher who is the chairman of the Language Department at St. Anne's School in Brooklyn Heights and teaches French literature there, she has also taught vast numbers of children—most of them between the ages of seven and twelve—how to cook beautifully, not just hot dogs and 'burgers but grown-up food, often French, always good. The children learned how to cook a meal without spending all day in the kitchen or too much money at the grocery store.

Happily, Colette's method is not just for children. Learning to cook the Colette way can help lots of other people: brides, bachelors, ex-husbands, women with jobs—as one newspaperman (Jay Sharbutt, Associated Press) put it, "adults who suffer stove fright and tend to exist on peanut-butter and honey sandwiches when nobody's around to cook for them."

More happiness: Colette's method is fail-safe. Everyone knows that self-confidence helps you to learn; using Colette's methods, you learn to cook *without failures.* You will learn each skill by taking just a baby step from the last one. When you have taken all the steps, you not only will be able to prepare all the basic dishes in this book but will be able *to cook any dish you choose from any other cookbook.* The secret is that Colette will have taught you all the skills and also taught you *how to read a recipe.*

Most cookbooks are catalogs of recipes; this one is a cooking course. Do not go through the book looking for a dish you like. You must begin at the beginning and study all of the recipes; that way, you will learn everything you need to know *in the right order.* Colette will tell you how to buy the ingredients, how to get them ready for cooking, and how to prepare the dish. She has said, "Preparation is the most enjoyable part of cooking. If children are too young to use the stove or oven, they can still have the fun of putting the dish together and the mother can 'cook' it." Because almost everyone likes to eat desserts, Colette begins her teaching in Chapter 1 with desserts and then goes on to things that are harder but even more fun, until, at the end of Chapter 6, you will have learned to cook a whole meal, including the appetizer, soup, main dish, vegetables, and salad, as well as dessert.

Because Colette and her architect husband, James Rossant, (they live in Manhattan) have four children (three of them girls and, last, a boy), most of these recipes are designed for six people. But cooking is an art, not a science; and not everyone eats the same amount, so you will have to be the judge of how many friends to invite to your "tastings." Tasting: That word is very important to Colette. In talking to young children she avoids the confusions of too much measuring by teaching them to "add a little and then taste." You can do that, too; but she has included amounts for the ingredients and told how to measure them.

When Colette is cooking with children, she often teaches them some French words; and they teach her some English ones. Since she can't consult her readers about language, she asked me to help in editing this book. I enjoyed it. You will, too. —L.J.D.

1 DESSERTS

I like meats and salads and soups and vegetables very much, but of all the parts of the meal I like the desserts best. After all, dessert is what you don't *have* to eat—but want to. Desserts can be delicious; they can be beautiful; and, sometimes, they can be quite spectacular. When I was a child in France, we had a wonderful kitchen, and I spent a lot of time there trying to sneak a finger into every single bowl I could find and to taste everything that was being made. But, of all the times I spent in the kitchen, I was the happiest when my grandmother and her cook were preparing a dessert. I was always given the spoon to lick.

Very early, as a little girl, I was also given things to do in the kitchen. I would beat the eggs; I would add the sugar, and sometimes even be given the caramel to do. And that was, for a small girl, a difficult task. Very soon, by the age of ten, I could cook a lot of desserts. I have taught my children how to cook desserts, too. They range in age from eight to sixteen; and they can all cook, and so can you.

Every country has desserts of some sort, but in many lands they are only served for special occasions. One exception is the

Middle East, where the people love everything that is sweet. Middle Easterners eat sweets all day long, especially very sweet candies like little cakes. At the end of the meal, they eat very, very sweet desserts—such as baklava, which is literally swimming in honey. When we were children, we spent the winter in Cairo; on Sunday afternoons, we used to go to visit my great-grandmother, who was Egyptian. She would receive us in a room covered with pillows. We used to sit on the pillows and, for the hours that the visit lasted, we would be stuffed with lucoum, honey cakes, baklava, and candy.

We used to sit on the pillows and be stuffed with candy.

In France, cakes, pies, creams, and ice cream are almost always served for very special occasions such as birthdays or parties or to delight a special guest. The French also eat cake on Sunday and for tea. Even though the French are world famous for their desserts, at the end of an ordinary meal, they rarely eat sweets. Instead, they eat fresh fruits—a bunch of grapes, apples, pears—always served with some cheese.

COOKING WITH COLETTE

In China, as in many other countries, dessert is not very important. After an everyday family meal the Chinese never eat elaborate desserts or cakes. Quite often they eat small pastries that are filled with lotus-seed or plum paste. And they eat one or two, never more. At Chinese banquets, a feast at which fifteen to eighteen dishes are served, they do have elaborate desserts; but these dishes are always very delicate. They might include a bowl of exotic fruits, little pastries filled with seed paste, delicate cakes made from the paste of fruits that is like a stiff Jell-O, or—something I love—roasted walnuts and almonds.

In South America, the family meal will never include fancy cakes or creams. The South Americans eat milk puddings—they are called *dolce de leche*—or another dessert, which is made of stewed fresh fruits, that is called *dolce delici*. They save the cakes for special occasions, and it is then that they serve the yummy fancy desserts.

The United States is different from these other countries. Here you can eat desserts every day, sometimes even twice a day. It's marvelous. When I first came here, I was amazed by the desserts you could get at a typical restaurant and at the elaborate sundaes you could get at a soda fountain. I gained fifteen pounds the first six months I was here. In the United States, you don't have to wait for a special occasion to cook a wonderful dessert; and there are many different kinds of desserts. In this chapter, I will tell you how to make cold desserts, hot ones, cakes, pies, and how to serve fruit. The recipes are mostly French ones, but the results will be sure to please everyone, no matter where you are.

Cooking desserts is fun. When you are cooking desserts, don't forget to leave the spoon in the bowl for others to lick; and don't forget to taste the raw dough. Raw dough is delicious. You get to taste everything as you go along. You have a chance to make something delicious to eat and lovely to look at; but, remember, recipes are only guidelines. In the beginning, it is best to follow the rules; but, as you go along and feel more sure of yourself, think of ways to experiment. You can substitute ingredi-

I gained 15 pounds the first six months.

ents; you can try new ways to make desserts look stupendous. Out of the few basic recipes given here, you can make I don't know how many different and wonderful treats. You will also learn how to follow other recipes in other cookbooks.

Before starting to cook, here are a couple of easy tips that you should know:

1. Measuring flour: To measure a cup of flour, choose a cup that does *not* have the cup mark below the top. Fill the cup with flour and bang it lightly on the table so that the flour settles. Fill it to the brim and level off, using a knife blade. If you are measuring less than a cup, when the flour settles straight across it should be level with the line on the measuring cup for the amount you want. For less than a cup, it is easier to use one of the smaller "cups"—for one-half or one-third, for instance.

If you have less than you want, take a spoon and add more flour and bang lightly again; and keep doing this until you have

COOKING WITH COLETTE

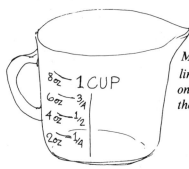

Measuring cup. Measuring cups have lines on them for one-quarter, one-third, one-half, and three-quarters of a cup; or there are separate cups for these amounts.

the desired amount. If you have more than enough, take your spoon and remove the extra flour. I never sift flour; I don't think it's as necessary with today's flour as it was in grandmother's day.

2. Measuring liquids: Measuring liquids such as water, oil, or melted butter is very easy. Use a transparent measuring cup, glass or plastic, with the lines clearly marked and the cup mark below the top. Leave the cup on the table or the counter top; then, pour the liquid directly into the cup until it reaches the line called for in the recipe.

When you measure water, it is much easier to pour it from a kettle into the measuring cup that is resting on the table top than it is to fill the cup from the faucet and to try to measure with your eye from that angle.

3. How to use measuring spoons: With measuring spoons, as with measuring cups, the correct amount is usually level or flat and straight across. If the spoon is too full, simply run a knife across the top to get rid of the excess.

Measuring spoons.

Sometimes recipes call for "heaping" teaspoons or table-spoons, which is exactly what it sounds like: Pile on as much as you can. "Rounded" is halfway between "heaping" and "level." If the recipe just says "spoon," it means "level."

Heaping teaspoon.

Sometimes recipes call for a "pinch" of something. If you were going to pinch someone, how much skin would you grab between your fingers? That's how much a pinch is.

4. Measuring butter: Measuring butter is easy, because in the United States the wrappers of most stick butter are marked with lines at each tablespoon. A stick of butter (¼ pound) is eight tablespoons. All you have to do is cut off the required amount of butter with a knife; do it *before* you unwrap the butter.

5. Melted butter: Melting butter is very simple, but there is one problem—butter burns. To make life easy, use a small pot, cut the butter into a few small pieces, and heat it over a low flame. One more thing: Keep your eye on it. If your butter burns, throw it out and start all over.

6. Melting chocolate: Melting chocolate isn't difficult; but, like butter, it burns easily. To make sure that the chocolate doesn't stick to the bottom of the pot, it is best to use a double boiler. Put some water in the bottom of a double boiler and wait until the water begins to simmer, which means that tiny bubbles begin to form.

Next, cut the chocolate into a few small pieces and put them in the top of the double boiler; then, put the top of the double boiler over the simmering water. Stir the chocolate constantly with a wooden spoon, so that the chocolate doesn't burn. You'll know when it is melted—take a taste, it's delicious.

7. To separate eggs: Many recipes tell you to separate eggs, which means that you must separate the egg white from the yolk. Before you start a recipe, practice separating eggs first. Take one, two, or even three eggs and two bowls, one for the yolks and one for the whites. Hold an egg in your hand and give it a slight tap on the edge of the bowl until the shell cracks slightly in the center. The shell is very fragile; don't tap too hard, because then you will break the shell completely. Once the shell is cracked, hold the egg in both hands and insert your two thumbnails into the crack. Holding the egg over the "whites" bowl, pull the two halves away from each other very gently, turning the egg to one side so that the yolk rolls into one half of the shell. That way, when you separate the two halves completely, one half of the shell will hold the yolk and half of the white; the rest of the white will be in the bowl. If you have done everything right (it usually takes a few tries), you now hold the two shell halves in your hands; pour the yolk into the empty shell, and let the white drip into the bowl. Keep pouring back and forth until all the white is in the bowl. Next, pour the yolk into the other bowl. It doesn't matter if the yolk breaks when you put it in the bowl, because it is going to get mixed up later on anyhow.

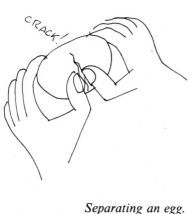

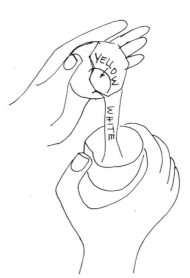

Separating an egg.

If something goes wrong, what do you do? Certainly, not worry. If you break the shell, use your hand and fingers. Fingers make a marvelous sieve. Put the egg into your hand, hold onto the yolk, and let the white drip into the bowl.

What if the yolk breaks completely into the white? Well, then you can't use the egg white, but you can make very good crêpes with the egg. (There is a crêpe recipe in this chapter.) If the yolk doesn't break completely, you can try to save the egg white by using a spoon and picking up as much of the yolk as possible.

Now, take a second egg and try it again. Did you do better this time? Take a third egg and try it once more.

8. To beat egg whites: Once you have learned to separate eggs, you have to learn how to beat them.

When beating egg whites, always add a pinch of salt. The salt helps the egg white to get stiff. Beat the whites with either a rotary hand beater or an electric egg beater. It is much more tiring to use a hand beater, but the results are sometimes better. You end up with peaks like mountain tops. With an electric beater, you will get a smooth mixture, and sometimes no peaks. No matter which method you use, the egg whites when cooked will taste the same.

Add a pinch of salt.

If you use a hand beater, always beat in the same direction. It doesn't matter which direction you start with, but don't change it and don't stop beating until the eggs are stiff. You will know that your eggs are ready by lifting up your beater. If the egg whites stay in the blades, you are finished. If the whites slide out, beat some more until they stay in the blades. By then, the bowl will look as though it is full of snow. Tap the blades on the side of the bowl, and turn the beater in the opposite direction from the way you were beating; the whites should just fall out into the bowl.

9. To beat egg yolks: For many desserts, you will beat egg yolks as well as egg whites. When you beat yolks, you always will add sugar as you go along. The recipe will tell you how much sugar to add. Before you add the sugar, beat the yolks until they are light yellow and slightly thick. Slowly, pour in the required amount of sugar as you keep on beating. The yolks are beaten enough when you lift up your beater and you have what looks like a thin yellow ribbon falling out of the blades.

10. To fold eggs: Often a recipe will tell you to fold the beaten yolks into the stiff beaten whites. Folding is similar to stirring only instead of going around the bowl you turn the

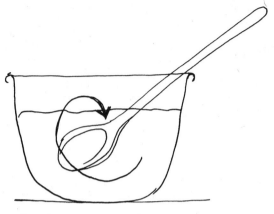

Circular motion.

mixture from bottom to top. To fold eggs, pour the beaten yolks
very gently into the beaten whites. As you pour, turn the mixture
lightly from the bottom over and over, with a circular motion of
your wooden spoon. When you fold, the ingredients don't have to
be very well mixed.

PIE AND FRUIT RECIPES

Before we start cooking, there are certain utensils you will
need to make these desserts. If a recipe requires different utensils,
these will appear at the top of the list of ingredients. In general,
this is what you need:

A measuring cup or cups
A measuring spoon or spoons
A couple of wooden spoons
Bowls of different sizes
Pie plates, usually 9″ in diameter
A mixer, either electric or a rotary hand one

Before you start to cook, read the recipe *all the way*
and make sure that you have *all* the equipment and ingr

Let's start by making dough. Dough is very versatile. It can
be used to make a dessert such as pie, or to wrap up fruit, or to
make a hot salted main dish, sometimes even to wrap up meat.
What is interesting to know also is that dough can be refrigerated
for a couple of days, or we can even put it in the freezer and use it
whenever we need it.

DOUGH

This is a basic dough that never fails. My grandmother, who
lived in Egypt, loved pastries and taught me how to make this
recipe. It literally never fails. You can use it to make pie or any
sweet dish that requires a dough, or you can make it salted. What
is very good about this recipe is that it is easy to remember. What
you need are equal portions of oil, hot water, and melted butter
and then as much flour as the dough needs. If it is a salted dough
we are making, a pinch of salt; if a sweet one, a little sugar. Now,
if you want to make a lot of dough, you increase the quantity. If
you want to make just a little bit, you diminish it.

Here is a recipe for dough, enough for two 9" shells. In
French, we call an open fruit pie *une tarte*.

WHAT DO YOU NEED?

4 tablespoons melted butter (or ¼ cup)
¼ cup oil (any vegetable oil)
¼ cup hot water
1 tablespoon sugar
2 cups flour

The easiest way to follow a recipe is to have your ingredients
ready. Therefore, have the water boiling, and have the flour, the
sugar, and the oil easily available. Melt your butter in a small pot,
as directed in the beginning of the chapter. Take a bowl, put in the

oil, the hot water, the butter, and the sugar and mix well with a wooden spoon. Add one cup of flour, mix the flour with the liquid with the spoon, add a second cup of flour, and mix it with your fingers. The flour should be completely incorporated in the butter, oil, and water. Make the dough into a ball, and dust your ball with flour. Let the ball of dough rest for 10 minutes.

If you have followed the recipe carefully, the dough should be very smooth. Now that you have the dough, let's start our first recipe—a pie.

PIE CRUST

Utensils needed: a pie plate, a rolling pin.

Heat the oven to 350°F.

Butter and flour the pie plate. How do you butter a pie plate? Take a little piece of butter and, with your fingers, spread it all over the pan, on the bottom and on the sides.

Take a tablespoon of flour, put it in the center of the pie plate, holding it over the sink—that is very important. You do not want to have flour all over the place. Shake the pan around to spread the flour so that all the pie plate is lightly covered with flour, and shake out the excess flour.

Dust your dough ball and your counter top with a table-spoon of flour each. Cut your ball of dough in two. If you are making only one *tarte,* refrigerate the extra dough to use later.

Roll the half portion of dough once with your rolling pin. Turn the dough around, roll it again; sprinkle the dough again with flour, and roll once more. Then, turn the dough on the other side; sprinkle it again with flour, and roll it once more. By now you should have a dough more or less the shape of a circle. It should be the size of your pie dish. Roll until the dough fits, but roll as little as possible.

Roll the dough the size of your pie dish.

Lift the dough onto your pie dish and, with your fingers, press all around so that the dough sticks to the edge of the pie dish.

With a fork, prick the bottom part of the dough in the pie dish; this will prevent the dough from bubbling. Put the dough in the 350° oven and bake it for about 25 minutes. After 20 minutes, check your crust. It should be a light golden color. When 5 minutes more are over, turn off your oven and take out your pie crust. Now that you have a pie shell, you have to fill it with some fruit, canned or fresh, to make it a French *tarte*. We can use canned fruit; this is the easiest thing to do. The following recipe is for stewed apricots.

APRICOT PIE

WHAT DO YOU NEED?

6 ounces raspberry jelly
Juice of ½ lemon
1-pound can apricot halves
1 baked 9″ pie shell

Empty the raspberry jelly into a pot. Cook it slowly on a low flame, stirring it with a wooden spoon. When it starts to boil, add the juice of half a lemon. Turn off the gas and let the jelly cool. Meanwhile, drain the apricot halves, place them in circles in your pie. When the raspberry jelly is cool to the touch, pour it over the apricots. Put the pie in the refrigerator for two hours. Serve it on a white dish. You will get compliments; it is really delicious.

If you like the apricot pie, and you want to experiment with fruits, you could use canned peaches, canned plums, or canned pears. Here is a recipe for fresh fruit.

APPLE TARTE

WHAT DO YOU NEED?

1 pound of apples, peeled and cored
1 baked 9″ pie shell
2 tablespoons brown sugar
1 teaspoon ground cinnamon
1 tablespoon butter

Light your oven and set it at 375°. Slice your apples very thin. Form circles of sliced apples in your pie crust. (See illustration.) Mix the brown sugar and the cinnamon and sprinkle over the apples. Cut the butter in small pieces, and sprinkle them over the pie. Put the pie in the oven for 10–15 minutes. Check it at 10 minutes; the butter should have melted with the sugar and formed a golden brown crust. Turn off the oven, cool the pie, and put it in the refrigerator for two hours. When the French want to make a more elaborate pie, they use at the bottom of the pie a custard called *crème anglaise*. The *crème* is cooked, separately, and poured into the pie; and on top of the *crème* one puts, usually,

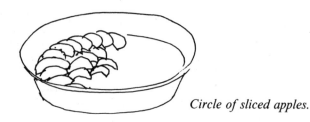

Circle of sliced apples.

fresh fruits. You can also use canned apricots or canned peaches. The *crème* pie is a little bit more difficult, but it is beautiful and extremely tasty.

CRÈME ANGLAISE

What is a *crème anglaise?* This is a custard sauce that is a blend of egg yolks, sugar, and milk cooked until it is thick. The only difficult part about making a *sauce anglaise* is that sometimes the eggs can scramble; therefore, always cook it on a low flame.

WHAT DO YOU NEED?

1 baked 9″ pie shell and fruit for your *tarte*
3 egg yolks
1½ tablespoons sugar
A pinch of salt
1 cup milk
1 teaspoon vanilla
And, if you want to, a tablespoon of brandy

Separate the egg whites from the yolks, following the directions on page 7. Refrigerate or freeze the egg whites; later on, we could use them to make a mousse. In a bowl, mix egg yolks and the sugar and the salt with a fork; don't beat them, just mix them well. In a heavy pot, heat the milk. When bubbles appear on the edge of the milk, slowly pour half of the milk into the egg mixture, stirring constantly with a wooden spoon. (If you don't do that, some of the eggs might suddenly cook.) Pour this mixture slowly back into the remaining milk and put the whole mixture into the top of a double boiler. The water underneath the double boiler must be boiling. Continue to stir the sauce with a wooden spoon. When the mixture thickens and coats the spoon, the *crème* is done. Then add the vanilla and the cognac. Cool the sauce for 5–10 minutes. When the pot is cool to the touch, pour the sauce into your pie crust. If you are using canned fruits, such as apricots, then put the apricots in a circle on top of the cream. They will sink slightly. Cool in the refrigerator for two hours.

STRAWBERRY TARTE
WITH CRÈME ANGLAISE

WHAT DO YOU NEED?

Crème anglaise (see recipe on page 15)
1 baked pie shell
2 ½-pint baskets of strawberries
½ 8-ounce jar raspberry jelly
An ordinary paintbrush or a pastry brush
Confectioner's sugar (optional)

Make your pie crust as you have done before. Then make your *crème anglaise*; cool it; pour it into the pie crust. Refrigerate the pie crust with the *crème anglaise* for two hours. Meanwhile, wash your strawberries with the stems still on; drain them. I have found that if you leave the stems on, water does not get into the strawberries, and they are never soft. Half an hour before you are ready to serve, hull your strawberries (pull off the stems and

This time they will stand on top of the crème.

leaves) and place them on your *crème anglaise* in circles, as you have done with the apricots. This time they will stand on top of the *crème*. (See illustration.) Melt your raspberry jelly in a pot; let it cool; and, with the paintbrush, brush the strawberries with the melted jelly. Refrigerate the pie again for 10 minutes, and you are ready to serve. Sometimes, I sprinkle some confectioner's sugar on top of the strawberries, about a tablespoon. The berries look like red peaks with white snow on them.

NOTE: You can replace the strawberries with any fresh fruit you like; my favorite one is fresh peaches, when they are in season. If you use fresh peaches, or fresh plums, they should be peeled and this is how you do it:

Have a pot of water boiling; spear your peach on a fork, and dip the peach into the boiling water for a few seconds. The skin will then come off very easily. Let the peeled fruits cool, and then slice them thin and form circles on top of the *crème*. Again use raspberry jelly.

You can also use ½ pint of blueberries on your pie. Wash and drain them and put them in a bowl with two tablespoons of sugar; mix well and let the berries stay in the refrigerator for an hour or more. As you are about to serve, put the blueberries on top of the *crème anglaise* and sprinkle them with confectioner's sugar. Don't use any raspberry jelly this time.

You have learned now how to make dough, pie crust, apricot pie, strawberry pie, or blueberry pie, *crème anglaise*. Now, you may have some questions. Something might have gone wrong. Here are a couple of questions and answers from mistakes I have made in the past.

What has happened, when I make the dough, if it is too dry and crumbles?

If you find that your dough is too dry and crumbles, for a full recipe (page 11), add one tablespoon of oil and one tablespoon of hot water; mix well. If it is still too dry, add another tablespoon of water.

What happens if I have too much dough? What can I do with it?

If you have any dough remaining after you have made your pie, roll it up in a piece of foil paper. It can stay in the refrigerator for two days. If you don't think you are going to use it within the next two days, then freeze it. When you defrost the dough, it might be dry; if so, again add a little oil and a little hot water.

What can I do with the remaining dough?

You could make an apple turnover by peeling an apple, coring it, adding in the center of the apple a piece of butter and a tablespoon of jam, and covering the apple with dough. To make your dough a golden color, take one egg, beat it with your fork with one tablespoon of water, and with your paintbrush brush the dough. Set the turnover on a buttered pie plate or piece of foil and bake it for 15–20 minutes at 375°. It makes a lovely snack.

Before we go on to other recipes, here are other ways to use a *crème anglaise.*

POACHED PEARS

WHAT DO YOU NEED?

**1 pear per person
2 tablespoons lemon juice
¾ cup granulated sugar
½ teaspoon ground cinnamon
2 cups boiling water**

Peel the pears, leaving the stems on. They look very nice in a dish; and, furthermore, you can hold the pear by the stem when you eat it—it doesn't roll on your plate. Put lemon juice, granulated sugar, cinnamon, and water in a heavy pot. Boil for a few minutes. Drop the pears in, one at a time and simmer for 10–15 minutes, or until they are tender when pierced with a fork.

Don't overcook the pears. Remove from heat and put pears (with syrup) in a round bowl, stems up, and let them cool. When they are cold, place them in the refrigerator. Serve them with a side dish of *crème anglaise*. You can do the same with any cooked fresh fruit, but remember the following things:

1. Apricots, peaches, and plums have to be peeled either before or after they are cooked and cooled.
2. Never overcook any fruit, it becomes like mush.

BANANA FLAMBÉE

If suddenly you have nothing in the house and no time to make a dessert, you can do this quickly if you have bananas.

Count half a banana per person. Slice the bananas lengthwise. Take a stick of butter. Melt the butter in a frying pan. When the butter bubbles, put in your sliced bananas, add two tablespoons of sugar. When the bananas are brown on one side, turn them over with a spatula and brown the other side, about 5 minutes. Bring the frying pan to the table, pour in two tablespoons of brandy and light it. You will find this is a delicious dessert.

POACHED FRUITS

Earlier in this chapter, you learned how to poach a pear. You can also poach peaches, plums, apricots.

Just remember that when you poach peaches, plums, or apricots, they are better if they are peeled. You can peel them before you poach them. To peel peaches, plums, or apricots you can dip them quickly in boiling water—the skin will slide off easily; or you can peel the fruits after they are cooked and cooled. To serve the poached fruits, put them in a glass bowl or in individual little dishes. They can be served with whipped cream or you can serve them with *crème anglaise*.

MOUSSE

Mousse may sound like an animal, but it is really a French word that means "moss"; and it applies to anything that is soft and very, very light. Have you ever walked along the beach after a storm and found white foam on the sand? Have you picked it up and found that it is light as air and full of bubbles? Or, have you taken a bubble bath and played with the bubbles? That's the consistency of a mousse. Basically, mousses are made with whites of eggs and heavy cream beaten very stiff; to these are added beaten egg yolks with some kind of flavor: chocolate, coffee, vanilla, etc.

COFFEE MOUSSE

I made this coffee mousse when I came home from work at five o'clock and found my daughter Marianne in a state of panic. She was going to her school for dinner and had promised to bring the dessert but had forgotten all about it. The only ingredients I had in the house were eggs, sugar, cream, and coffee; and we turned out the most marvelous coffee mousse in 10 minutes.

WHAT DO YOU NEED?

4 egg whites
1 pint heavy cream
½ cup sugar
2 tablespoons instant coffee
Boiling water
1 envelope Knox gelatin
2 tablespoons cold water

Separate egg whites from the yolks (see page 7) and beat the whites very stiff. Then, pour heavy cream in a larger bowl and beat; when halfway beaten, add ½ cup of sugar slowly while beating. The egg whites and the heavy cream should be very stiff. Fold the egg whites into the heavy cream (see page 9). Have some hot water boiling. Put the instant coffee in a bowl, dissolve with three tablespoons of boiling water. Then, empty the envelope of Knox gelatin into another bowl. Add two tablespoons of cold water to soften the gelatin, then quickly add the gelatin to the hot coffee to dissolve. Don't wait. The gelatin gets hard very quickly. The next step is to add the coffee mixture into the egg–cream mixture. Fold it in, one tablespoon at a time, until your mousse is a light coffee color. Pour it into a serving dish. It's nice, if you have some coffee-bean candies, to sprinkle a few on your mousse; or take a piece of sweet chocolate and grate it over the mousse, just to give it some color. Refrigerate the mousse for two hours, and serve. It is really delicious.

The same mousse can be done with many fresh fruits.

CRANBERRY MOUSSE

Cook one pound of cranberries with ¾ cup of sugar, ¼ cup of water. Add one envelope of Knox gelatin soaked in cold water, as you did before, to the hot cranberries. Cool the cranberries, save about one cup for decoration, and fold in the remaining cranberries to the egg white–cream mixture and refrigerate the mousse for two hours.

RHUBARB MOUSSE

This is my favorite mousse. You need one pound of rhubarb washed and cut in 1″ pieces and cooked with ½ cup water and ½ cup sugar. (Don't taste the rhubarb leaves—they are poisonous.)

Cook the rhubarb until it falls apart and looks like lots of little strings. Then add to the rhubarb one envelope of soaked Knox gelatin; cool the mixture. Finally, fold the rhubarb into the egg–cream mixture—be careful not to beat it, just gently fold; and refrigerate it for two hours. You will find out that this is an excellent recipe.

From now on you can experiment with many other fruits or many other flavorings such as vanilla or rum mousse. The only time I have failed with this recipe is when I have used blueberries. Somehow the color of a blueberry mousse is very unappetizing.

Remember always to decorate your mousse. It makes your dish look so much more elegant. With the cranberries, always save a handful of the cooked cranberries and sprinkle them on top of the mousse. Or, for the rhubarb, I have often used thin slices of lime placed in a circle or in the center of my mousse. It did look beautiful.

CHOCOLATE MOUSSE

This is one of the most exciting of cold desserts. It is beautiful to look at and it is lovely to serve at the end of a good meal. It is slightly more difficult than the other cold mousses you have done so far; but by now you should be an expert in separating eggs, beating them stiff, and folding them with whatever flavor you have been using.

WHAT DO YOU NEED?

A double boiler
6 1-ounce pieces of Baker's semi-sweet chocolate
⅓ cup cold water (or cold milk)
¾ stick butter (or 6 tablespoons)
4 egg yolks
5 egg whites
1 cup sugar
A pinch of salt
1 tablespoon brandy (optional)
1 envelope Knox gelatin (optional)

Heat water in the bottom pot of a double boiler until it starts simmering. Break the chocolate into small pieces and put them in the top part of the double boiler. Add one-third of a cup of cold water (or cold milk, if you prefer). Melt the chocolate, stirring constantly with a wooden spoon. When the chocolate is melted, take the pot off the stove, add the butter a little at a time. The first two pieces of butter will be difficult to mix in, but as you add more butter the mixture will be easier to handle. Mix well. Remove from the hot water.

Separate your eggs into two bowls (see page 7). You need four yolks and five whites, so refrigerate one yolk in a covered dish with a little oil. When you have separated the egg yolks from the whites, take the bowl with the yolks and start beating. As you beat, the yolks will change color. Pour in, slowly, the sugar. Keep beating until the yolks change from a bright yellow to a light yellow—until they look like a pale-yellow ribbon spilling from the beater.

Pour the beaten egg yolks slowly into the chocolate, stirring all the time. Put the pot back on top of the double boiler and beat for a few more minutes so that the mixture is smooth and full of little bubbles of air. Then, take the top pot off the water and let it stand to cool for 5–10 minutes.

Add a pinch of salt to the egg whites, including the extra egg white; beat until the whites are very stiff and stay in the blades when you lift up the beater.

Take the chocolate mixture and very slowly fold it into the beaten egg whites (see page 9). In other words, pour the chocolate mixture into the egg whites and turn the mixture with a wide movement of your wooden spoon, starting from the bottom to the top. Don't try to mix it *too* well; it is nice to have some of the white peaks showing. If you want to add anything extra, like a tablespoon of brandy, don't be afraid—it won't really taste of alcohol. Add it now and fold it in.

If, for some reason, your mixture seems to be too soupy (it has happened to me quite often), take an envelope of Knox gelatin, put it in a bowl, add one tablespoon of cold water. Get a small pot and put three or four tablespoons of your chocolate mixture in it; add the soaked gelatin, and boil the mixture on top of the stove so that the gelatin is all melted; combine with original chocolate mixture and cool thoroughly. Slowly fold this final mixture into your egg whites and cream until it is well mixed, and refrigerate.

Pour this mousse into a nice-looking mold or bowl, or into little individual pots, and put it into your refrigerator for at least two to three hours. It will even be better if you leave it overnight.

If you want to be very impressive, you can add other flavorings that you like such as one teaspoon of vanilla, or two tablespoons of orange liqueur, or you can sprinkle roasted almonds on top of your mousse; or, add ¼ cup of grated orange rind, or anything else that you think goes well with chocolate.

You also can mold a mousse, but it must have gelatin in it to be molded, so follow the last step if you plan to use a mold. Take the mold, put some cooking oil on the tip of your finger, and oil the entire inside of the mold. Pour the chocolate mousse into the mold, and leave in the refrigerator overnight.

The next day, take the mold out of the refrigerator and run a knife around the edge to loosen the mousse. Fill up the sink with hot water; and, just before you serve the mousse, dip the mold quickly for a second only into the hot water. Be careful not to let any water run over into the mousse. Take a large plate, put it on top of the mold, hold them tightly together, turn upside down together, and PLOOP—the mousse will slide out onto your plate, and it will be in whatever shape the mold was. Now you have something truly beautiful. You can serve it with whipped cream, or you can put slices of orange all around it, or anything that you think will make a nice colorful arrangement around the chocolate mousse.

SOUFFLÉ

Another cold dessert that is very exciting, beautiful to serve, and excellent to taste is a cold lime soufflé. If limes are not in season, a cold lemon soufflé is equally delicious. Or, if you would like to try to make an orange soufflé, use oranges instead; but don't use as much sugar as the recipe calls for, because oranges are much sweeter than limes or lemons. Instead, add sugar to taste.

This soufflé is really a "mock" soufflé; it doesn't have to be cooked, and instead of its rising we make it look as if it has risen by filling the bowl to the edge. Once the soufflé has set, the dessert will look light and airy, just like a real soufflé. A soufflé is very like a mousse, which is also very light and will melt in your mouth. Soufflés can be served hot or cold. When they are made with sugar, they are desserts; made with salt instead, with cheese, or vegetables, or fish, they are served hot as a main course.

LIME SOUFFLÉ

WHAT DO YOU NEED?

A 2-quart soufflé dish
A double boiler
4 egg yolks
½ cup lime juice
½ cup sugar
½ teaspoon salt
1 envelope Knox gelatin
¼ cup cold water
1 tablespoon grated lime rind
6 egg whites
1 cup heavy cream
1 lime, sliced

The recipe calls for more egg whites than yolks, so, when you separate your eggs, put the extra yolks into a dish with a little oil in it and put it in the refrigerator. You can use the yolks later to make crêpes or whatever.

Take two bowls and separate your eggs (see page 7). Heat some water in the bottom of the double boiler until it begins to simmer. Grate the lime rind and squeeze the juice. Put four of the egg yolks in the top of the double boiler, add the lime juice, the sugar, and salt. Put the top of the double boiler over the simmering water, stirring the mixture with a wooden spoon until it mixes well and begins to thicken and stick to your spoon. Don't let the mixture get too hot or burn. When the mixture is thick, remove the pot from the hot water.

Soften the gelatin as you have done before in one-quarter cup cold water, and stir it into the lime mixture. Add at least a tablespoon of grated lime rind to the mixture. The more grated lime you add, the tarter your soufflé will be. You can add as much or as little as you like; but I think it is best with a lot of skin, a whole rind or even two rinds. Mix everything with your wooden spoon until it is well blended. Let the mixture cool.

Beat the six egg whites until they are very stiff. In another bowl, beat one cup of heavy cream until stiff. As with egg whites, when the cream gets stiff and full of peaks, you know it's ready.

Fold the heavy cream into your egg whites. Once that's folded, take the lime mixture and carefully fold that into the egg-white mixture. Pour the mixture into a soufflé dish. Refrigerate it for at least three hours.

Before you serve the soufflé, cut a lime into very thin slices and remove the pits; decorate the soufflé with a circle of lime slices. Or take some green leaves from a house plant (be sure it's not a poisonous one) and make a design on your soufflé. Or put a cherry in the middle to add some color. When you finish you will have a magnificent dessert that everyone will enjoy.

Take some green leaves from a house plant.

Now that you have made a cold lime soufflé let's make a hot lemon one.

HOT LEMON SOUFFLÉ

WHAT DO YOU NEED?

2 bowls
A 2½-quart soufflé dish
7 egg whites
6 egg yolks
½ cup sugar
A pinch of salt
Rind of two lemons
Juice of two lemons
Confectioner's sugar

Separate seven eggs; you'll have the yolks in one bowl and the whites in another (save one yolk for another use). For this recipe, it would be easier if you use an electric beater. Beat the egg yolks until they are very thick and a very pale yellow. Gradually beat in the sugar and a pinch of salt. Beat the mixture until it is very thick and very smooth. Add the grated rind and the juice of two lemons.

Whip the seven egg whites until they hold definite peaks. Gently fold the whites into the yolk mixture and pile the mixture in your soufflé dish.

This soufflé has to cook in a *bain-marie*. What is a *bain-marie*? A *bain-marie* is a pan sitting in another pan of hot water in the oven.

Stand the soufflé dish in a shallow baking pan of hot water and bake the soufflé in a moderate oven, 375°, for 35–40 minutes. Do not open the oven door for the first 30 minutes. You will know the soufflé is ready when, opening the oven gently, you see that your soufflé has risen and is cracked in the center like an open fruit. Sprinkle the soufflé with confectioner's sugar and serve immediately.

The difference between a hot soufflé and a cold soufflé is that the hot soufflé will flatten out very quickly. Therefore, you must serve it as soon as it comes out of the oven.

BLUEBERRY SOUFFLÉ

Now you have succeeded with your soufflé; that was an easy soufflé. Here is another one that is a real soufflé; which means that once you understand the basic recipe, you will be able to make a soufflé of any flavoring you wish. The most important part of this recipe is what we call in French a *roux*. A *roux* is a mixture of flour and butter that is cooked with milk to make a sauce. This is, with the egg whites and the yolks, the basic recipe for any soufflé; it can be made for a cheese soufflé, a vegetable soufflé, a chocolate soufflé. What we are going to do now is a blueberry soufflé. Once you have succeeded with the following recipe, you will be able to cook from any cookbook; or use your imagination, and make a soufflé of any flavor you wish.

1 small saucepan
1-quart soufflé dish
3 tablespoons butter
3 tablespoons flour
¾ cup milk
4 egg yolks
¾ cup sugar, plus extra sugar
A pinch of salt
1½ cups blueberries
1 tablespoon brandy or cognac
5 egg whites
Confectioner's sugar

The roux: In a small saucepan, melt three tablespoons of butter. Remember, butter burns easily; have a low flame underneath the saucepan. Stir three tablespoons of flour into the butter, and mix it up quickly. This is your *roux.* When the flour-butter mixture becomes like a ball, move the saucepan away from the fire and pour the milk in slowly, stirring constantly. When all the milk has been absorbed by the flour, put the saucepan back on the flame and cook all this, stirring constantly, until it is smooth and very thick. You may have lumps in the beginning. If you do, before adding all the milk, try to dry up the sauce by stirring it constantly until all the milk is absorbed by the flour. Then take the rest of the milk and slowly again add the milk to the *roux,* stirring it constantly. If you have not succeeded don't worry. Here is a trick to save your sauce: Take a very fine sieve, and pass the sauce into another saucepan through the sieve; all the little lumps will stay in the sieve. Take your wooden spoon and mash them through the sieve. Put the saucepan back on the low fire. When the sauce is thick, remove the pan from the heat and let the white sauce cool.

DESSERTS   **29**

You have separated four eggs. In a bowl, beat the egg yolks thoroughly and slowly add the sugar. Then stir them into the white sauce. To that white sauce add the blueberries and one tablespoon of cognac or brandy.

Separate the last egg. Then beat five egg whites with the salt until they hold definite peaks. Carefully fold about one-third of the egg whites into the blueberry mixture, mixing it thoroughly.

Add the remaining whites, folding them *very lightly and very gently.*

Butter the soufflé dish and sprinkle it with sugar, as you did before, when you were making a pie, with the flour. Pour the mixture into the soufflé dish and bake the soufflé in a moderately hot oven, 375°, for 30–35 minutes. Do not open the door for the first 30 minutes. When the soufflé is done, quickly take it out of the oven. Dust the surface with confectioner's sugar and serve. Remember, the soufflé must be served immediately.

NOTE: If you are not very sure a soufflé is done, here is a little idea that I use quite often. When your soufflé has been in the oven for about 30 minutes, open the oven and, from the side, poke a clean knitting needle into the soufflé. If the needle comes out clean, the soufflé is done. If the needle does not come out clean, let the soufflé stay in the oven for another five to ten minutes.

CRÊPES

Every country in the world has pancakes. In Russia, they are called *blini;* and they are stuffed with caviar or sour cream. In China, they use very thin pancakes and stuff them with a dish called "mushi pork." But of all the pancakes, the undisputed crown prince is the French *crêpe.* A crêpe makes a fabulous dessert. It is a very, very thin pancake with edges that look like lace. What make the crêpe the best of all pancakes are its delicate texture and the ease with which it can be rolled and folded; even when served in a sauce, the crêpe is never soggy. The crêpe can come to a table as an hors d'oeuvre, or as a main dish stuffed with very savory fillings, or as a dessert with fruit sauce or butter sauce and gloriously flambée with brandy.

Crêpes is a dessert that all children love to make in France. The time that we do it most is the first Tuesday in January; it is a holiday in France that very much resembles the American Hallowe'en. We all dress up in costumes and go to one another's houses and play games. And whoever has a party makes a big batch of crêpe batter, and then everyone goes to the kitchen and makes crêpes. You have to flip them, and flip them as high as you can, and catch them back in your pan, and not drop them on the floor. The one who manages to make the most crêpes and flip them the highest gets the prize, which is either a toy or a bag of candy. When I was a child, it was a silver coin.

Flip them as high as you can.

OH LA LA!

CRÊPE BATTER

The following recipe is the basic batter for crêpes. Once you learn how to make your crêpes, you can serve them any way you want and use your imagination for the filling.

WHAT DO YOU NEED?

A 7-inch iron or aluminum skillet
4 eggs
1 cup flour
½ teaspoon salt
1 cup milk
1 cup water
2 tablespoons melted butter, plus some extra

In a bowl, beat four whole eggs until they are well mixed, and add the flour with the salt. Beat the mixture until it is very smooth. Add gradually the milk, water, and melted butter. Stir the batter until it is well blended and has the consistency of heavy cream. You cannot use the batter immediately; it has to stand for at least 30 minutes. And I usually let it stand for one hour.

Heat your skillet until it is very hot and brush it with some melted butter. Pour in about three tablespoons of the batter and remove the pan from the heat; turn the pan around to distribute the batter evenly. Bring the pan back to the heat, cook the crêpe until it is light brown on the bottom. Carefully, with a knife, separate the edges from the pan. Move the pan away from the heat, tilt it, flip the crêpe over, put back on the heat to brown the other side. Continue making crêpes in this manner, and stack them to keep them moist until all the batter is used. This recipe will allow you to make sixteen to eighteen crêpes.

Very often you will not be successful with the first few crêpes. You have a lot of batter, and you can practice. If you want to learn how to flip them, here is a little secret. As you take the knife and separate the edge of the crêpe from the edge of the pan, tilt your crêpe pan and with the knife push the crêpe to the upper edge; then flip it.

If you are not going to use the crêpes immediately, instead of stacking them one on top of the other, separate each crêpe from the next with a piece of waxed paper.

HOW TO SERVE THE CRÊPES

One of the simplest ways to serve crêpes is to sprinkle them with sugar and eat them as you make them.

CRÊPE FILLING

WHAT DO YOU NEED?

Crêpes
½ stick butter
Any jam
Juice of one lemon
Confectioner's sugar

Once your crêpes are made, put a teaspoon of jam on each crêpe and spread it. Sprinkle a little bit of lemon juice, a little bit of sugar, and roll the crêpe. Put it on the serving plate. Pour a little bit of melted butter on top and sprinkle with sugar; serve immediately.

CRÊPE FLAMBÉE

WHAT DO YOU NEED?

Crêpes
A heavy skillet
1 stick butter
4 tablespoons sugar
Juice of 1 orange
3 or 4 tablespoons brandy

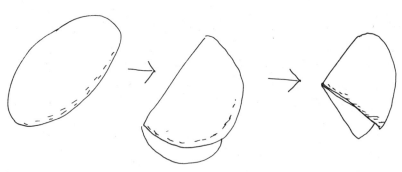

Fold the crêpes.

This is a spectacular one. And it is really easy to make. Fold the crêpe as illustrated. In the skillet, melt your butter. Stir in the sugar and the juice of the orange. Put the folded crêpes in your skillet. Heat. Turn them over once. Bring the pan to the table. Pour in the brandy and light it. It is a magnificent dessert.

Once you have done these few recipes for crêpes, dozens of other ideas for filling the crêpes will come to your mind. Any sweet thing you like can be put in the crêpe, and in Chapter 2, on hors d'oeuvres, you will see that we can fill them with meat, fish, etc.

PÂTE À CHOUX

Pâte à choux is a French dough that is cooked on top of the stove and then baked; and, like crêpes, it can be used as a dessert, filled with whipped cream or lemon custard, or glazed with caramel and served with hot chocolate sauce. Or, as a main dish, it can be stuffed with meat or fish or shrimps or lobster.

PÂTE À CHOUX DOUGH

Pâte à choux is very easy to make and is, like crêpes, very versatile.

WHAT DO YOU NEED?

Pastry sheet
Paintbrush
1 cup water
1 stick butter (½ cup), plus extra butter
1 teaspoon sugar
1 cup flour
4 eggs
1 tablespoon water

In a heavy saucepan put the water, the butter cut in small pieces, the sugar; and boil the mixture at high heat. Lower the heat, and add—all at once—the cup of flour. With a wooden spoon, beat the mixture until it leaves the side of the pan and forms a ball. Keep on turning this ball until it is completely loose. You know it is ready when, if you were to turn the pot upside down, the ball of dough would fall (but don't try it). Remove the pot from the heat. With a wooden spoon crack three eggs. Add one egg at a time. The secret of the *pâte à choux* is that each egg has first to be mixed thoroughly before you add another one. The batter should be just thick enough to hold peaks. If, after adding the three eggs, the batter is still too stiff, break another egg; beat it in a bowl; and add as much of the beaten egg as is necessary to bring the batter to the right consistency.

Now you are ready to bake your *pâte à choux*. The *pâte à choux* cannot wait; it must bake soon after it has been cooked.

Butter a large pastry sheet. Sprinkle it with flour. If you have a pastry bag, fit it with a ½″ plain tube, fill the pastry bag with the *pâte à choux,* and pipe out eighteen little puffs, each about the size of a walnut and one inch high, onto the pastry sheet, leaving space around each puff for expansion. If you do not have a pastry bag, use a measuring spoon, a teaspoon, to form balls and drop them onto the pastry sheet. Break an egg into a bowl, add a tablespoon of water, and beat with a fork. With your brush, brush each little puff lightly with this egg mixture.

Bake the puffs in a heated oven, 425°, for 20 minutes. They are ready when they are light brown and crispy. Take the puffs out of the oven; make a slit in each one with a knife; and return them to the oven, with the heat this time turned off. Leave the door of the oven ajar, and let the puffs stay in the oven for 10 minutes; transfer them to a rack and let them cool. Now you have eighteen puffs, golden brown and crisp. You have to stuff them. You can stuff them with many different things. One dish, called in French *profiteroles*, is *pâte à choux* covered with caramel, stuffed with whipped cream, and served with a hot chocolate sauce.

PROFITEROLES

To make a caramel:

WHAT DO YOU NEED?

1 cup sugar
¼ cup water
⅛ teaspoon cream of tartar

In a heavy skillet, cook the sugar, water, and cream of tartar over moderately high heat until the mixture is a light caramel color. Be careful: Sugar tends to burn. Watch it constantly. You know the caramel is done when, with a wooden spoon, you stir the caramel, drip a drop of caramel onto a piece of waxed paper, and the caramel gets hard.

Transfer the caramel to a small shallow bowl. Dip the top of each puff into the hot caramel, being careful not to let any drip on your fingers. Hot caramel can burn you. Stand the puffs upright on a rack and let them cool.

Now let's make the *crème chantilly.*

WHAT DO YOU NEED?

1 cup heavy cream
3 tablespoons confectioner's sugar
1 teaspoon vanilla

In a bowl, beat the heavy cream until it's almost stiff, add the confectioner's sugar and the vanilla, and continue to beat. Just before you are ready to serve, carefully cut off the caramel top of each puff. Fill the puff with the whipped cream and put back the caramel top on the puff. Arrange the puffs on the dish, and serve them immediately with the hot chocolate sauce.

Hot chocolate sauce:

WHAT DO YOU NEED?

A double boiler
8 1-ounce squares semi-sweet chocolate
½ cup strong coffee

In the top of the double boiler, set over hot water, melt the squares of chocolate (cut into small pieces) with the strong coffee. Keep the sauce warm over the hot water until you are ready to serve. If the sauce becomes too thick you can add ½ stick of butter, cut into little pieces, or a little bit more coffee, or water; and if the dinner is served for guests, a tablespoon of cognac will make the sauce even nicer.

CAKES

SWISS CHOCOLATE CAKE

When I was a little girl and spent the winters in Egypt, I had a Swiss nurse. She was very tall and very, very strict. We didn't like her very much, my brother and I; and she knew it. One day she surprised us. She made a Swiss chocolate cake. It was so good that it broke the ice between Mademoiselle (this is what we called her) and us. Today my youngest daughter, Cécile, loves to make that cake because her favorite thing in life is chocolate. This cake has no flour; we often do it on birthdays.

How Mademoiselle broke the ice.

9″ round cake pan, 1½″ deep
Oil
Waxed paper
4 ounces semi-sweet or dark sweet chocolate, grated
1⅔ cup ground blanched almonds, plus extra whole or ground almonds
5 tablespoons fine dry bread crumbs, plus extra crumbs
1 tablespoon baking powder
1 stick butter (½ cup)
1 cup sugar
6 eggs
2 tablespoons cognac or brandy (optional)

The day you decide to make this cake and before you start working, take the butter out of the refrigerator and put it in a bowl to get soft. Preheat the oven to 350°. You will have to grate the chocolate. If you have a good blender, cut the chocolate in small pieces and put it in the blender with the blanched almonds. Blanched almonds are almonds that have no skin. You can buy them in little plastic bags. Or you can buy shelled almonds and dip them quickly in boiling water, drain them, and the skins will slide off easily.

Put the almonds and the chocolate in the blender. Blend until they are in fine crumbs. In a bowl, combine the chocolate, the nuts, the bread crumbs, and the baking powder. Work the butter with a wooden spoon until it is soft and creamy. Gradually, to the butter, add the sugar; and beat the mixture until it is light. To that mixture, add the chocolate-nut-crumb mixture and the brandy if you wish.

Separate the six eggs. Add one egg yolk at a time to the batter, beating each time. In a bowl, beat the egg whites until they hold definite peaks; then fold them gently into the batter.

Oil the cake pan; line the bottom with waxed paper, and oil the paper. Sprinkle the bottom and the sides of the pan with fine dry bread crumbs. Spoon the batter into the pan and bake the cake at 350° for about one hour, until it is done. (Use knitting needle to test it.) When the cake is done, take it out of the oven and cool for about 10 minutes before you remove it from the pan.

CHOCOLATE GLAZE

WHAT DO YOU NEED?

A double boiler
4 ounces semi-sweet chocolate
¼ cup water
½ stick butter (¼ cup)
¼ cup confectioner's sugar

In the top of the double boiler, set over simmering water, melt the chocolate, cut in little pieces, with the water. Remove the pan from the heat and add the butter in little pieces, stirring until it is all melted. Add the confectioner's sugar, and beat the glaze until it is smooth.

Pour the chocolate glaze over the top of the cake in one pouring and tip the cake back and forth so that some of the glaze runs down and covers the sides. Sprinkle the top and the sides of the cake with ground or whole almonds. You have now the most stupendous chocolate dessert you have ever eaten.

COFFEE CAKE

WHAT DO YOU NEED?

**9″ × 5″ loaf pan
Oil
½ stick butter (¼ cup)
¾ cup sugar
1 egg
⅓ cup fresh-brewed coffee
⅓ cup light cream
½ teaspoon vanilla
1½ cups flour
2 teaspoons baking powder
¼ teaspoon salt
1 teaspoon cinnamon**

The day you decide to make this coffee cake, and before you start working, take the butter out of the refrigerator and put it in a bowl to get soft. Preheat the oven to 375°. Then with a wooden spoon, work the butter until it is very soft and creamy. Gradually add ½ cup of the sugar. Make the mixture as smooth as possible. Add the egg, the coffee, the cream, the vanilla. Mix again very well. Add the flour and the baking powder and the salt. And stir it all into the creamy mixture.

Oil the loaf pan well. Pour the batter into the pan, and sprinkle the top with the rest of the sugar and the cinnamon.

When your oven is at 375°, bake the coffee cake for 30–35 minutes. Test it after 35 minutes to see if it's done, using your knitting needle, as you have done before with the hot soufflé. If the needle comes out clean, turn off the oven and cool the cake on a wire rack for about 5 minutes. Then remove it from the pan. Serve the cake with ice cream, or as a snack.

FRESH FRUIT SERVED AS A DESSERT

When fruits are in season and they are fresh and juicy, they are lovely served as a dessert.

How to choose and buy fruit: In the spring and in the summer, peaches, cherries, strawberries, and blueberries are plentiful; and they are refreshing to serve after a meal on a hot summer day.

Peaches: When you go to the market to buy peaches in the United States, they are often quite hard. If you want to serve the peaches as a dessert and they are hard, they should be poached (see pages 18–19). If the peaches are ripe when you buy them, be careful that they have no bruises. A peach should be red on one side and a bright yellow, or a golden yellow, on the other. Wash the peaches and serve them in a bowl; or, if they are big, they look lovely in individual dessert dishes.

Cherries: When I was a child we had a house in the country with three or four cherry trees. In June, when their cherries were ripe, there would be an outing for the whole day; we would have ladders, and we would climb on top of the ladders with baskets and pick the cherries. I must say that we all ate them very fast, faster than we put them in the baskets. The most beautiful ones were kept with their stems on and were steeped in good brandy for a special treat. Some of them we used to cook, poached in red wine; but I used to like to eat them fresh. My mother would take a very big woven basket and fill it up with cherries; and when the meal was over, the basket would be put in the center of the table. We children finished it very quickly.

When you go to the supermarket to buy sweet cherries, be careful that they are not bruised. They should be a brilliant or dark red and they should be firm to the touch. Wash them well. Leave the stems on. And put them in a bowl in the refrigerator.

Strawberries: In the United States, strawberries are plentiful. You can eat them nearly all year round. When you buy strawberries, they are usually sold in a small pint basket. Sometimes they are bruised underneath; always lift up the basket and look to see if there are bruised strawberries.

When you serve strawberries, you first have to wash them well. Remember, don't take off the stems before you wash them. Wash the berries with the stems on, then remove the stems. Put the strawberries in a bowl, sprinkle them with sugar, add a teaspoon of brandy or any liqueur you like; serve cold. You can also serve the berries with whipped cream or *crème chantilly* (heavy cream whipped with confectioner's sugar and a little vanilla).

Blueberries: Wash the blueberries carefully, drain, and put them in a bowl; sprinkle with sugar and refrigerate for a couple of hours. As with the strawberries, you can also add a teaspoon or a tablespoon of brandy to your blueberries.

Grapes: These are one of the loveliest fruits to see and the tastiest to eat. In the United States there are as many different kinds of grapes as in Europe; choose the kind you like best. To buy grapes, select them when they are fresh, plump, well-formed, and very firmly attached to the stem. Avoid grapes whose general appearance is shriveled, sticky, or dull. Wash the grapes thoroughly, drain, and refrigerate. If the bunches are very big, take scissors and cut them into two or three smaller bunches.

Mixed fruit: What is also nice to serve as a dessert is a mixture of fruit. Take a big platter or a basket. I like to serve my fruits in baskets. Start with the hard fruits, such as apples, oranges. I also put a pineapple in the center of the basket. Surround the apples and the oranges with peaches, plums, apricots. Sprinkle the whole basket with sweet cherries, sometimes having cherries hanging from the leaves of the pineapple. Also include a couple of lemons and limes; the yellow and the green make a marvelous splash of color.

WATERMELON BASKET

For the last recipe of this chapter, let's make a spectacular mixed-fruit dish that will serve ten or twelve people: it's a watermelon basket.

WHAT DO YOU NEED?

A melon-ball cutter
1 medium-sized watermelon
Fruits of your choice
1 cup sugar
¾ cup water
2 cups dry white wine
Confectioner's sugar

Watermelons are plentiful in the United States. Choose a medium-sized melon, and with the sharp tip of a knife score a two-inch-wide band crosswise in the center, stopping about one-third of the way from the top. Leave that band intact and slice in horizontally from each side until you reach the bottom of the band; remove the two side pieces. You can cut the top edge of your "basket" in a scallop design.

With a melon-ball cutter, scoop out the balls from the melon pieces, from the "basket," and from its "handle"; put them in a large bowl. You can add to that as many fruits as you want. For example:

Add two cups each of strawberries and raspberries, one cup of blueberries, some seedless grapes, two bananas peeled and sliced, one or two oranges peeled and sectioned.

In a saucepan, dissolve one cup sugar in ¾ cup water, over very low heat. Increase the heat to high, and boil the syrup for 5 minutes. Let the syrup cool, and add two cups of any dry wine you have. Pour the syrup over the fruit, and toss the mixture lightly. Transfer the fruit to the watermelon basket and chill the basket. Sprinkle the fruit lightly with confectioner's sugar, and serve. At the end of a summer meal this is a lovely dessert.

2 APPETIZERS— HORS D'OEUVRES

What is an appetizer? An appetizer is something you serve at the beginning of the meal. It is something that will make you want to eat more. Above all, an appetizer is something that is a lot of fun to do, because it requires a lot of imagination. Many of the recipes you learned as desserts are useful for appetizers, too, by leaving out the sugar and adding salt and a different flavoring. And, with some basic recipes, you can develop all sorts of appetizers on your own.

An appetizer is something cold or hot. It's something light or quite substantial. If the main course of the dinner is filling, then you will want to serve a light appetizer. If, on the contrary, there is a light main course, then your appetizer can be quite spectacular and substantial. Many of the appetizers in this chapter can easily be served as the main course at lunch or for brunch.

One of the main things you have to remember for all these appetizers is that they have to be beautifully decorated—always served on a nice dish. You have a wide choice of things you can decorate your appetizers with—parsley, watercress, hard-boiled eggs, aspic, olives, radishes, etc.

By now you have learned how to make dough and make pies. The following recipes use pie crust, but this time you have to omit the sugar and replace it with ¼ teaspoon salt.

QUICHE

A *quiche* is a mixture of eggs with cream, milk, and bacon (like a *quiche Lorraine*), or cheese, tomato, onions, fish, or anything that can be combined with eggs and poured into a pastry shell; it is baked in an oven and puffs up and browns. You can never miss with a quiche, and it is delicious for the beginning of a meal.

QUICHE LORRAINE

This dish is very easy to make, and what is interesting about it is that you don't have to do all the work at meal time. You can bake the pie crust, prepare your filling, and refrigerate your filling for a couple of hours. Half an hour before dinner, you pour the filling in the shell and bake the quiche. It will be ready and beautiful.

WHAT DO YOU NEED?

Half-baked pie crust
6–8 slices of bacon
3 eggs
1 cup heavy cream
1 cup milk
½ teaspoon salt
A pinch of pepper
1–2 slices Swiss cheese, broken in pieces
1–2 tablespoons grated Parmesan or Romano cheese (optional)
1 or 2 teaspoons butter, cut into small pieces (optional)

Make your pastry according to the recipe on page 11; make the pie shell with half the pastry, refrigerate the rest to use later. Follow the directions on page 12 in preparing the shell. Bake the pie shell for 10–12 minutes. Take it out of the oven and let it cool. Fry your bacon in a frying pan until it is light brown. Dry it on a paper towel. Break it into small pieces and sprinkle it on the bottom of the pie shell. In a blender mix the eggs, the cream, the milk, the salt, the pepper, and add the Swiss cheese. When the mixture is well blended, you may refrigerate it until you are ready to bake. Heat your oven at 375°. Pour the filling into the pie shell. Bake the *quiche Lorraine* for 25–30 minutes. After 25 minutes check it by using a knitting needle. If the needle comes out clean, your quiche is ready. It should be golden brown and all puffed up.

Sometimes, to make my filling even more tasty, I add to the egg mixture one or two tablespoons of grated Parmesan cheese or Romano cheese. I also add the pieces of butter on top of the egg mixture before I put the pie in the oven. The butter makes the mixture even richer. You have to serve the *quiche Lorraine* soon after it cooks; if not, it will go down.

You can keep a *quiche Lorraine* by freezing it, or you can serve it cold on a picnic. When you're going to use it cold, then do add the grated cheese. Cold, the *quiche Lorraine* is much tastier with Parmesan cheese. You can replace the bacon with ham; you then will have to cut the ham into small slices or into cubes. You can also use ham and bacon together. You can add sliced mushrooms if you are using the quiche for a main course at lunch. It will make the *quiche Lorraine* even more substantial.

The mushrooms: Wash three or four large mushrooms very well. They always have sand in them. Never peel the mushrooms, but take the ends of the stems off. Rinse the mushrooms in a bowl of water with a tablespoon of vinegar; dry them well. Cut them in small pieces or slice them; cook them lightly in a tablespoon of butter. When they are halfway cooked, add them to your egg mixture and finish the *quiche Lorraine* as you have done before.

QUICHE AUX OIGNONS (ONIONS)

Mademoiselle, our Swiss nurse (who taught me how to make the marvelous Swiss chocolate cake that I hope you have already baked), also used to make a *quiche Lorraine* with onions. It is lovely to eat as an appetizer. I also serve it for lunch.

WHAT DO YOU NEED?

1 half-baked pie shell (see page 12; bake 10–12 minutes)
5 or 6 large onions
1 tablespoon oil
3 tablespoons butter
1½ tablespoons flour
2 eggs
⅔ cup cream
1 teaspoon salt
A pinch of pepper
½ cup grated Swiss cheese

Peel the onions. Now, peeling onions often makes people cry. There is really no real way of peeling onions without crying. Some people say that if you peel onions under cold running water it will help. I find that if the onion is strong, really nothing helps. Just cry and wipe your tears. Chop the onions very fine, which means slice the onions one way first and then the other way. (See illustration.)

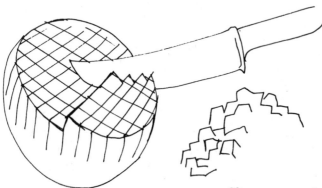

Slice one way, then the other way.

Put your finger in the mixture.

You should have about five cups of chopped onions. Cook the onions in a frying pan with the oil and the butter on very low heat. Stir occasionally until the onions get a golden color. When they are ready, sprinkle the onions with the flour and mix well. Cook slowly for 2–3 minutes; then let cool. In your blender, put your eggs, the cream, the salt, pepper, the grated cheese; blend well. When the mixture is blended, add the onions. Remember always to taste what you are cooking. Put your finger in the mixture, lick it, see if there is enough salt and pepper; if not, correct the seasoning. Pour the mixture in the half-baked pie crust. Bake the tart in a preheated oven at 375° for 35–40 minutes until it is golden brown and all puffed up.

I have found that the onion quiche takes longer to cook than a regular quiche.

SAUCISSON EN CROÛTE

This is a very delightful hors d'oeuvre. It is a sausage cooked in a dough and served hot with mustard. In France, Italy, and New York you can find the right sausage. It is called in the United States *cotechino*. It is a big, fat, uncooked garlic sausage. It is Italian. The French have a similar one. If you cannot find it in your neighborhood, you can use the Polish sausage. It doesn't taste quite the same, but it is also quite good. Or you can make your own sausage. Following is the recipe for *saucisson en croûte*, using a *cotechino* you purchased or one you made yourself. It is fun to make your own sausage.

WHAT DO YOU NEED?

Dough for the crust (see page 11)
1 *cotechino* (about 1½ pounds)
1 egg
1 tablespoon water

Take your *cotechino* and put it in a heavy pot. Cover it with water and let it simmer, covered, for 45 minutes. Remove the sausage and let it cool. With a knife, make a lengthwise slit in the skin. Remove the skin.

Make your dough by the recipe on page 11, omitting the sugar and adding ½ teaspoon salt. On a floured board, roll the dough ¼" thick. Place the *cotechino* in the center of the dough and wrap it. How do you wrap? Roll one side of the dough over the sausage, and then the other. Cut the excess dough off. Seal the dough along the seam and at the ends by dipping your finger in cold water and wetting one edge of the dough. Beat an egg slightly with one tablespoon of water. Brush the dough with the egg mixture. Heat your oven at 375°. Take a shallow pan, butter it well or spread with a tablespoon of oil; put the wrapped sausage in the pan. Bake the sausage for 25 minutes, until the dough is golden brown. Serve on top of lettuce. Slice the sausage about an inch thick, and serve it with French mustard and French bread.

Make your own sausage:

WHAT DO YOU NEED?

Dough for the crust (see page 11)
½ pound veal, ground
½ pound pork, ground
¼ pound pork fat, chopped
2 egg yolks
¼ teaspoon each: dried tarragon and parsley
2 cloves garlic
Salt and pepper
Pistachio nuts (optional)

In a bowl, mix together the veal, the pork, and the fat. Add one of the egg yolks. Add the tarragon and parsley. Chop the garlic fine and add it to the mixture. Add salt, pepper, and, if you want, a little package of shelled pistachio nuts can be added.

When you're done, shape the meat mixture in a roll like a sausage. Put it in the center of the dough. Roll the dough around the meat and proceed as in the previous recipe. Heat your oven at 375° and cook the *saucisson en croûte* for at least 40–50 minutes, until the dough is golden brown and until the meat is cooked. Serve it hot, sliced an inch thick, with mustard.

CHEESE SOUFFLÉ

You have done soufflés as desserts before. A hot soufflé, with salt instead of sugar, is basically the same thing. It is made with eggs in a sauce and the whites of eggs beaten very stiff. The basis of the soufflé is the sauce made from a *roux,* which you learned to make on page 29. The white sauce is one of the most important things in cooking. This simple sauce is the basis of a lot of sauces, such as *béchamel,* which is a white sauce, and *crème velouté;* and it is often used as the basis of cream soups. The sauce is not difficult to make, but it requires quite a lot of practice.

The basic idea of the *roux* is to cook the butter and the flour slowly for several minutes before any milk or bouillon is added to them. To make a *roux* it is best to use a heavy-bottomed enamel or stainless-steel saucepan. If you use a thin saucepan, you will burn the *roux* very quickly.

WHAT DO YOU NEED?

2 tablespoons butter
3 tablespoons flour
2 cups milk (or bouillon)
¼ teaspoon salt
A pinch of pepper

You can replace the milk with bouillon made with chicken or beef bouillon cubes. To make a soufflé, it is best to use milk.

In the saucepan melt the butter over low heat. Pour the flour in all at once and cook it slowly, stirring continuously until the flour gets a slight brown color. Remove the *roux* from the heat and, stirring constantly, add the milk very slowly. Don't worry if you have lumps. As soon as you see that lumps are forming, put back the saucepan on very low heat and cook until the flour is dry again. Remove the saucepan from the heat and continue to add the milk very slowly, stirring vigorously all the while. When you have added all the milk, set the saucepan over moderate heat again and stir until the sauce comes to a boil. Boil gently for one minute. Turn off the heat, and add the salt and pepper. Taste to see that the seasoning is correct. This sauce is the basis for a soufflé; to it we can add whatever flavoring we wish. The following recipe, for a cheese soufflé, is the basic recipe for any soufflé. Remember, use your imagination to change the flavoring.

To make a soufflé you need a soufflé dish. A soufflé dish is often made out of porcelain or Pyrex. This recipe requires a six-cup soufflé dish, which is about 3½ inches in height and about 5½ inches in diameter. You can also use individual soufflé dishes, which are much smaller. Before you start the recipe, butter the soufflé dish very well. Take a tablespoon of flour and sprinkle it inside the soufflé dish, shaking the dish so that all the sides and the bottom are covered with the flour. Throw out the excess flour.

WHAT DO YOU NEED?

A 6-cup soufflé dish
2 cups white sauce (see above)
4 egg yolks
5 egg whites
Salt
¾ cup grated Swiss cheese or a mixture of grated Swiss and Parmesan cheese

Make the sauce following the preceding recipe. Remove from the heat. Separate the eggs. Drop the whites into the egg-white bowl and the yolks into the center of the warm sauce, one at a time. Beat each yolk into the sauce with a wire whisk. Continue until you use up four of the egg yolks (save one). Taste the sauce again. Add salt, but not too much, because Swiss cheese and Parmesan cheese are salted to begin with. Let the sauce cool. Preheat the oven to 375°.

Meanwhile, beat the egg whites with a pinch of salt until they are very stiff. Stir into the sauce two tablespoons of the egg whites; then add the cheese. The next step is delicate. Do it carefully. Delicately fold the egg sauce into the stiff egg whites (reread the directions on page 9). Do it carefully. Don't overmix, or the egg whites will collapse and your mixture will be liquid. Pour the mixture into the floured dish; it should be about ¾ full, because a soufflé rises. Sprinkle some grated cheese on top of the mixture. With your oven at 375°, bake the soufflé for 25–30 minutes until it is well risen and the top is golden brown.

Here's a little secret. To succeed with a soufflé, people usually say, "Don't walk in the kitchen, don't bang anything." All this is nonsense. The only thing is, don't open the oven door for the first 20 minutes. It will cool the oven and the egg mixture will fall. After 25 minutes, open the oven slightly and look at your soufflé mixture. It should really have risen, the center should have

Don't walk in the kitchen.

cracked like an overripe fruit, and it should be golden brown. Another secret—your soufflé has to be served immediately. Soufflés are very light and they fall very quickly. If you are not sure your soufflé is done after 25 minutes, you can take your knitting needle and put it through the center of the soufflé. If the needle comes out clean, the soufflé is ready. A soufflé should not be overdone, because it would be all dried up.

This is the basic recipe for a soufflé. You can make any soufflé you want by changing the flavoring of your white sauce. You can add vegetables, fish, seafood, etc. Following is a recipe for a vegetable soufflé. You can also make a chicken soufflé—it needs more spices. Seafood soufflés are delicious. Meat soufflés are not quite as good.

SPINACH SOUFFLÉ

WHAT DO YOU NEED?

6-cup soufflé dish, buttered and floured (see page 52)
1 pound spinach, picked and washed
1 tablespoon minced shallots
1 tablespoon butter
¼ teaspoon salt
Pepper

2 cups white sauce (recipe, pages 51–52)
⅓ cup grated Romano cheese

Buy fresh spinach (see page 109 for some tips). Remove the stems and wash the leaves well. Dry them in a towel. You can also use frozen spinach. If you use frozen spinach, let it thaw and drain well; dry with a towel.

Peel and chop the shallots. Shallots are little brownish-gray onions; you can find them in some supermarkets or at a greengrocer. Melt the butter in a frying pan, and sauté (stir-fry) the shallots. Don't overcook them.

Chop up the spinach and add it to the frying pan. Add salt and pepper, and cook the vegetables over moderately high heat for several minutes until all the water has evaporated. Spinach is a vegetable that can be cooked with almost no water, because it contains so much water itself. Once the spinach and the onions are cooked, remove from heat.

Prepare the soufflé base (sauce recipe on page 52); and, after the egg yolks have been beaten into the white sauce, add the spinach and shallots. Taste to see if the mixture needs salt or pepper. Beat the egg whites very stiff (with a pinch of salt). Add the cheese, minus one teaspoon, to the egg mixture. Add 1 or 2 tablespoons of the beaten white to the egg-spinach mixture, and then fold that mixture into the egg whites. Pour into the prepared soufflé dish. Sprinkle with remaining cheese. Bake in the oven at 375° for 25–35 minutes.

You can also make this recipe with cooked broccoli or carrots, chopped fine or puréed in the blender.

OTHER SOUFFLÉS

Using the same recipe as you did for the spinach soufflé, you can make a number of variations: Replace the spinach with ham—⅓ cup of chopped boiled ham, along with 2–3 tablespoons of chopped, sautéed mushrooms. Or you can replace the spinach with a 7-ounce can of salmon or crab meat, drained.

When I make a salmon soufflé or a crab-meat soufflé, I drain the can of salmon or crab meat and keep the liquid as a base for my white sauce. Sometimes you do not have enough of the salmon or crab-meat liquid, especially crab meat. The salmon liquid should make about half a cup; add half a cup of milk. Add the salmon or the crab meat to your egg-yolk sauce and continue as for any other soufflé.

If you have any cooked chicken or cooked turkey, grind the cooked poultry, and add it to your egg-yolk mixture. It makes a very nice soufflé. Make your spices a little bit stronger. Add more salt and pepper, and a little tarragon or oregano.

PUFF PASTRY (PÂTE À CHOUX) SERVED AS AN APPETIZER

You have made *pâte à choux* as a dessert. Now you can use the same *pâte à choux* combined with cheese or filled with shrimps or meat or tuna as an appetizer.

CHEESE PUFFS

WHAT DO YOU NEED?

Dough for *pâte à choux* (see pages 34–35)
¾ cup grated Swiss cheese
Deep-fat fryer and thermometer
Vegetable shortening and cooking oil

Make the *pâte à choux* as you have done in the chapter on desserts, pages 34–35. When the dough is ready, stir in the grated

Swiss cheese. Taste the dough. It should be salty and peppery even when you taste it raw.

In a deep fryer, heat enough vegetable shortening and oil (in equal amounts) to be about 3 inches deep. Use a deep-fat thermometer to test the temperature. When the oil is hot (375°), dip the bowls of two tablespoons into the oil and use the oiled spoons to shape 1½-inch balls of the dough. Lower the balls into the fat and fry them, three or four at once, turning them several times, until they are lightly brown. They will "explode" in the fat and double in size. Drain the puffs on paper towels, and serve them hot with a tarragon sauce.

TARRAGON SAUCE

This sauce uses the white sauce you have just learned to make.

WHAT DO YOU NEED?

1 cup dry white wine
2 tablespoons dried tarragon
2 tablespoons minced shallots
1–2 tablespoons soft butter
2 cups béchamel (white) sauce (see pages 51–52)
½ cup heavy cream (optional)
4 tablespoons fresh chopped parsley (optional)
Chopped fresh tarragon (optional)

In a small saucepan, put the wine, dried tarragon, shallots. Cook on a low heat until the volume is reduced to about three tablespoons of wine. This is called herb essence. It is very strong. Make your béchamel sauce the same way you have done previously for the soufflé (see pages 51–52). Add the herb essence; and, if you find that the sauce is too thick, add half a cup of heavy cream; then add the butter. Just before serving stir in the sauce the fresh parsley and, if you can get it, some chopped fresh tarragon.

CRÊPES

You have made crêpes as a dessert; crêpes can be used endlessly as an appetizer or as a main dish for lunch. They can be stuffed with shrimps, mushrooms, ham, chicken, cheese, or anything that comes to your mind once you have learned some basic ideas of how to fill and serve crêpes as an appetizer.

CRÊPES FILLED WITH
CHEESE AND MUSHROOMS

Make your crêpe batter as you have done for the dessert (see page 32). Do not add the sugar. Add instead ¼ teaspoon salt. Make ten or twelve crêpes and stack them. Cover them with a wet cloth to keep them moist.

Cheese and mushroom filling:

WHAT DO YOU NEED?

9″ round baking dish
1 cup cottage cheese (or 8 ounces cream cheese)
Salt and pepper
1 egg
¼ pound mushrooms, cleaned and chopped
1 tablespoon chopped shallots
1 tablespoon butter, plus extra butter
½ tablespoon oil
3 tablespoons grated Parmesan cheese

Mash the cottage or cream cheese with the salt and the pepper; stir in the egg.

In a frying pan, sauté the mushrooms and the shallots in the butter and oil for 5–6 minutes, until the shallots are golden brown. Stir them into the cheese mixture. Taste it to see if it has enough salt and pepper.

Butter a 9″ round baking dish and center a crêpe in the bottom. Spread a layer of cheese and mushrooms, and spread another crêpe, and continue until you have used up all the crêpes and the cheese mixture. Sprinkle the top of the last crêpe with the grated Parmesan cheese and 3–4 pieces of butter. Bake in an oven (350°) for 10–15 minutes; cut in wedges and serve very hot.

CRÊPES WITH HAM AND CHEESE STUFFING

Make the crêpe batter and prepare the crêpes as you have done before. You should have about ten or twelve crêpes.

Filling:

WHAT DO YOU NEED?

Shallow baking dish
1 tablespoon minced shallots
2 tablespoons butter, plus extra butter
1 cup minced ham
2 cups béchamel (the white sauce that you made for your
**   soufflé; see pages 51–52)**
½ cup grated Swiss cheese
Chopped parsley
Pieces of butter

In a small frying pan, sauté the shallots in the butter; mix in the ham. Add the mixture to the béchamel. Add all but a tablespoon of the cheese.

The white sauce should be quite thick. Take a shallow baking dish and butter it well. Place a tablespoon of filling on the lower edge of one crêpe, and roll up the crêpe into a cylinder. Repeat until all are filled. Arrange the filled crêpes in the baking dish. Sprinkle them with parsley, pieces of butter, and a tablespoon of grated cheese. Heat in the 350° oven for about 15 minutes—or until they are hot.

BRIE CHEESE CRÊPES

Brie is a French fermented cheese that is soft and has a crust; you can buy it many places in America now. The brie for the crêpes should be very runny, with the inside like thick cream that runs out of the crust. You must remove the crust before you use the cheese in the crêpes.

Make twelve crêpes and keep them warm, using the recipe and instructions on pages 32–33.

WHAT DO YOU NEED?

Shallow baking dish
½ pound brie cheese (at room temperature)
6 tablespoons béchamel sauce (see recipe, pages 51–52)
Pepper
3 tablespoons grated Gruyere and Parmesan cheese
3 tablespoons melted butter, plus extra butter

Butter a baking dish. Mash the brie into the béchamel sauce. Add pepper. Spread the cheese sauce on the crêpes and roll them. Arrange the rolled crêpes in a flat baking dish, sprinkle with the Gruyere and the Parmesan cheese, and pour over the melted butter. Heat the oven to 400° and bake the crêpes until the cheese is melted and the crêpes are lightly brown.

CRÊPES FILLED WITH SHRIMPS

This is a more elaborate crêpe filling, but it is also very tasty. You need fresh shrimps for this. Good quality fresh shrimps are firm to touch and have a fresh, slightly sweet smell. You can also use frozen shrimps; but they are neither as tasty nor as tender as fresh ones.

How to clean fresh shrimps: For best results, you should clean the shrimps before cooking. Hold the tail end of each shrimp in your left hand; and, with your right hand, slip your thumb under the shell between the feelers and lift off segments of the shell. When half the shell is off, pull the rest of the shell off the tail. Then you have to devein the shrimps. On the curved side of each shrimp is a black vein just under the surface. With a sharp knife cut about ⅛ of an inch deep along the outside curve. Then lift out the black vein. Wash the shrimps under running water; drain well.

Shrimp filling for crêpes:

WHAT DO YOU NEED?

2 tablespoons butter
2 tablespoons chopped shallots
1 pound shrimps, cleaned and deveined
Salt and pepper
1 teaspoon dried tarragon
½ cup white wine
Extra butter
1 tablespoon grated cheese
Tarragon sauce
1 teaspoon lemon juice

In a heavy saucepan, melt the butter. Add the chopped shallots. Cut the shrimps in small pieces, and add them to the shallots. Sauté lightly for 2–3 minutes until the shrimps turn a light white-pink. Add salt and pepper. Sprinkle with tarragon. Add the wine. Cook until the wine has nearly evaporated. Your shrimps are ready.

Make twelve crêpes (see page 32). Butter a flat baking dish. Spread some of the shrimps in the middle of each crêpe. Roll them and arrange in the baking dish. Sprinkle the crêpes with butter and a tablespoon of grated cheese. Bake in a hot oven (400°) for 10–15 minutes, until the cheese has melted and the crêpes look brown. Serve with the tarragon sauce (recipe on page 57) that you have previously made. To that sauce add 1 tablespoon lemon juice.

ASPIC

What is aspic? An aspic is a jelly that is crystal clear and as delicate in texture as in flavor. Its primary function is not so much to satisfy your appetite as to make a dish look more beautiful. Food coated with aspic often seems as if it were floating in space, and it gives the impression of an elaborate dish even when the food is simple.

Aspic is easy to use, because today we have instant gelatins that come in packages. Years ago, aspic took hours to make. You had to make the jelly by cooking bones for hours, clarifying the bouillon, and then keeping it in the refrigerator or some cool place. Today, aspic is quick and easy to do and can be used for beef and veal and chicken and fish. In my aspics, I always use a tablespoon of brandy or some white wine. That gives the aspic a better flavor.

There are several things you have to remember about aspics. One: Aspic should be spooned over the food when it is cold but still liquid. If the aspic is already set, you have to reheat it to melt it. Two: You should use one envelope of Knox gelatin for every cup of liquid you use. Three: Never pour aspic over *hot* food. It would take hours to chill, and the liquid would get into the food and you will never have the transparent, clear aspic that makes food so stupendous.

Always decorate your aspic. You can decorate it with thin slices of hard-cooked egg white; with pimentos that you get in jars or cans; with green or black olives that have been pitted; with the green part of scallions; with fresh twigs of tarragon; with carrots, raw, thinly sliced; with cucumbers, with the skin on, thinly sliced; or anything else you can think of. Aspic can also be used as a garnish itself. If you want to use aspic as a garnish, you pour it in a pan about an inch deep. Let it set. Then you coarsely chop it with a damp butcher knife and arrange it around any cold food you like to serve.

One of my favorite recipes for an appetizer is eggs in jelly. They are lovely to look at. And even if you don't like eggs too much, this is a marvelous appetizer. Everybody seems to enjoy it.

OEUFS EN GELÉE
(EGGS IN ASPIC)

WHAT DO YOU NEED?

6 French egg molds or individual baking dishes
3 cups boiling water
3 chicken bouillon cubes
1 cup tomato juice
4 envelopes Knox gelatin, softened
Salt and pepper
2 tablespoons cognac
6 poached eggs
Garnishes: tarragon leaves, cooked egg whites, olives
6 slices boiled ham

In a saucepan, boil 3 cups of water. Add three bouillon cubes. When the bouillon cubes are dissolved, add the cup of tomato juice. In a small saucepan, combine the four envelopes of Knox gelatin with two or three tablespoons of cold water. When the gelatin has softened, add it to the hot bouillon. Cook, stirring constantly, for 2–3 minutes until the gelatin melts and the stock boils again. Season. Strain the mixture through a very fine sieve and add the cognac. You will have about four cups of liquid aspic.

Poach six eggs. If you don't have an electric poacher, here is a way of poaching eggs:

Fill a wide 3″-deep pan ¾ full of water. Add two tablespoons vinegar. Bring the liquid to a boil, lower the heat to the simmering point. Crack the eggs, one at a time, into a small saucepan or a cup. Slide them gently into the simmering water, one at a time. As the egg hits the water the white has a tendency to spread. With a spoon gently bring back the white on top of the yolk. Let each egg simmer for 3–4 minutes. Remove each poached egg (as it is finished) with a slotted spoon and lower each quickly in a pan of cold water. Let the eggs cool in the water until they are completely cold. Remove the eggs, put them on a paper towel, and gently dry them. With a round cooky cutter, cut the edge of the white. The egg should now have its original shape.

Now you have your poached eggs and your liquid aspic. Oil six French egg molds or individual baking dishes. Spoon a thin layer of chilled, but still liquid, aspic into each egg mold. Chill. When the aspic is set, take your garnish—tarragon or white of egg or black olives—and dip the tarragon, or whatever you are using for decoration, into the liquid aspic and decorate the bottom of each mold. You can make a flower, using the white of egg for the petals, a black olive slice for the center. You can make a design with parsley or tarragon leaves. Chill again. Place one egg, yolk down, in each mold and cover with an oval of thin sliced ham. Fill the molds with chilled but still liquid aspic. Chill for a couple of hours until the aspic is well set.

To unmold the eggs in jelly, dip the outside of each mold quickly in a pan of warm water and turn out on a serving dish. Garnish the dish with watercress and aspic chopped up, or with slices of tomatoes, slices of radishes, anything that will make your eggs in jelly look even more beautiful.

HAM MOUSSE

Here is another recipe using the aspic you've just learned how to make. This is a superb dish, fit for a king.

WHAT DO YOU NEED?

3 tablespoons finely chopped scallions
1 tablespoon butter
2 cups chicken bouillon (made with cubes)

2 tablespoons tomato paste
2 envelopes Knox gelatin
¼ cup sherry
3 cups ground cooked ham
Salt and pepper
A grating of nutmeg (optional)
1 cup heavy cream
Aspic (see pages 62–63)
Garnishes: black olives, egg whites, etc.

In a saucepan, cook the scallions in butter until they are soft, but don't brown them. Boil two cups of water. Add two chicken bouillon cubes. When the cubes are dissolved, add this chicken stock to your saucepan. Then add the tomato paste, just to give it a nice pink color.

Soak two envelopes of Knox gelatin in ¼ cup sherry. Add the softened gelatin to the stock and simmer for 1–2 minutes. Remove from the heat and add the ham. Season the mixture well with salt and pepper. Add a dash of nutmeg—if you like nutmeg. Let the mixture cool. Meanwhile, beat the heavy cream until it is very stiff. Fold the whipped cream into the cold ham mixture (directions on page 9). Put the mixture in a bowl and put it in the refrigerator until it is nearly set. This will take about an hour.

Meanwhile, make an aspic, following the previous recipe on page 63. When the aspic is cool, rinse a 6-cup mold (I use a shell shape) with cold water. Cover the bottom with a thin layer of cool, but still liquid, aspic and chill the aspic until it is firm. Decorate the edge or bottom of the mold with a circle of hard-cooked egg whites. In the center of each circle put a piece of black olive or, if you can afford it, a piece of truffle. Pour a little bit of thin liquid aspic on top of the decoration and chill again. When the aspic is set, carefully fill the mold with the ham mousse (spoon it in), and cover the ham mousse with the rest of the liquid aspic. Chill it for several hours in the refrigerator. The best thing is to let it stand in the refrigerator overnight. When you are ready to serve, unmold the mousse by separating the edge of the mousse from the mold with a knife and dipping the mold quickly in hot water, then put a platter face down over the mold and, holding them tightly, turn upside down. Surround the mousse with parsley, and serve it with thin, toasted white bread. You will get only compliments for this fabulous dish.

PÂTÉS

Pâté is one of the glories of French cuisine. Each province, each town, each French woman, has a special recipe for pâté. It is not an inexpensive dish, but it is a dish that will keep for one, two, sometimes three weeks in the refrigerator and can be served on any occasion. In general, pâté contains ground meats, such as pork, veal, chicken, duck. The French even make a pâté with wild boar and squirrel. Don't say "ugh!" It is superb.

Don't say "ugh"!

Very often pâtés are made of goose liver. Goose liver is very difficult to find in the United States. In France, they put geese in little cages and overstuff them, until their livers become enlarged; and this is the liver that is used to make fabulous goose-liver pâtés.

Very often also, in the pâtés, you will see truffles. A truffle is a fungus, a round dark-brown ball with a thick wrinkled surface. I read once that in the Middle Ages the truffle's appearance gave rise to a belief that truffles were formed from witches' spit, which was believed to be dark in color, rather than the white of a normal human being. Most truffles weigh a few ounces; but sometimes they are quite big, reaching two and a half pounds.

Finding a truffle is quite an experience. They live and grow underneath oak or beech trees, and they give off a smell that human beings cannot detect. Animals love the smell of truffles, and farmers and other hunters use animals to find the truffles. In Russia, they have tried to use little bear cubs; and it is said that in Siberia they employ goats; but the French most of the time use pigs, and sometimes dogs. It takes a long time to train a pig to hunt for truffles but not to eat them.

Today, truffles are so expensive that they are truly a luxury. To replace the look, but naturally not the taste, of truffles in pâtés that I make, I use black pitted olives.

To bake a pâté, you need a baking dish: a special rectangular mold that the French call *terrine,* or you can use a soufflé dish, a casserole, a bread pan—I use a cake pan sometimes. Some of the *terrines* are spectacular. They can be made of china or pottery; they have beautiful birds or roosters, usually, or the head of a duck, on the lid.

The principle of this pâté, and usually of most pâtes, is that meat, highly seasoned, is arranged layer upon layer. This one has a layer of sausage, a layer of veal, a layer of chicken livers, a layer of pork; and then we start all over again. Each meat is prepared separately and then the layers are formed.

WHAT DO YOU NEED?

1½ pounds Italian sausage
½ teaspoon sage
Salt and pepper
1½ pounds ground veal
1 egg
3 teaspoons dried tarragon
1 slice white bread
¼ pound pork fat
6–10 chicken livers
¼ cup cognac
1½ pounds ground pork
3–4 teaspoons chopped fresh parsley, plus extra parsley
2 or 3 shallots, chopped
2 chicken breasts, boned
2 thin slices bacon
Garnishes: olives, pistachios, carrots, hard-cooked eggs
2 envelopes Knox gelatin
2 bouillon cubes
1 teaspoon soy sauce

To prepare layers:

Sausage meat: The Italian sausage comes in casings. With the point of a knife, break the casings, and remove the sausage. To the sausage meat, add ½ teaspoon of sage, salt and pepper, and mix well. Let it stand.

Veal: To the veal, add the egg; two teaspoons of dried tarragon; salt and pepper; the slice of white bread soaked in a little bit of water, the water being squeezed out of the bread. Veal can be dry, so we add fat. Pork fat can be bought in the supermarket; if it's salt pork, you have to boil it in water for 5–10 minutes to remove the salt. Chop the pork fat very fine, and add it to the veal. Mix very well. Taste it—it should be highly spiced.

COOKING WITH COLETTE

Chicken livers: You have six to ten chicken livers, whole. Remove any veins that you can find. Add a teaspoon of dried tarragon, salt and pepper, and ¼ cup of cognac. Let the livers marinate. Cognac that you use for your pâté can be cheap brandy used for cooking. It does not have to be an expensive brandy that is used to drink.

Pork: To the pork, add salt and pepper, one or two teaspoons of chopped fresh parsley. Take two or three shallots, chop them fine, and add them to the pork. Taste. It also has to be quite spicy.

Chicken breasts: You can de-bone your chicken breasts, or you can buy them already boned in the supermarket. If you are boning the breast, cut it in two in the center and pull out the bones. It is really very easy. Cut the chicken meat in very thin strips. Add salt and pepper, two teaspoons of fresh chopped parsley, and let it stand.

Now that your meats are all ready, what you have to do is make layers of them. At the bottom of your *terrine,* or cake or bread pan, put two thin slices of bacon. Add half the sausage. Flatten it well, then add a layer of half of the chicken strips. On top of the chicken, add the veal, always using half the mixture. Then take your chicken livers and put them in the center of the pâté, in a line. At this moment you can decorate your pâté with other things, such as black olives, or green olives stuffed with pimento. Pistachio nuts are very good. Anything that, when sliced, will give a color. Then add half the pork, and start all over again. End up either with the pork or the sausage. Cover the top of the pâté with foil, so it is well sealed, but make a hole in the center for the steam to get out.

Heat your oven at 400°, and bake your pâté for an hour and a half, in a *bain-marie* (see page 28). When the pâté is done, remove it from the oven and, leaving it in the pan and without removing the foil, put cans of vegetables or a pot filled with water, anything that will serve as a weight, on top—so that the meats will be compressed; then, when you slice it, the pâté will not fall apart. Let stand in the kitchen overnight.

The next day, remove the foil and now it is time to decorate your pâté.

First, pour off all the liquid in the pan. Use olives, carrots, hard-boiled eggs, or parsley to form flowers or designs on top of the pâté.

Soak two envelopes of Knox gelatin in a tablespoon of cold water. Add two cups of boiling water. Add two beef or chicken bouillon cubes and stir until dissolved. Add a teaspoon of soy sauce to give your jelly a nice color. Cool. Pour ½ the cold but still liquid jelly around the pâté (the pâté will have shrunk away from the pan while cooking). Put the pâté and the rest of the aspic in the refrigerator until the aspic has half set. Then spoon the aspic on top of the pâté, so that the top of the pâté will also be covered with gelatin. Refrigerate the pâté for at least two to three days before you serve it.

To serve the pâté, you can either unmold the pâté and put it on the platter surrounded with lettuce leaves and some chopped-up aspic, or you can serve it thinly sliced, on a bed of lettuce leaves, with white buttered toast. It is a very festive pâté. You can eat it with mustard, or just plain, or serve it with a tomato salad.

PÂTÉ EN CROÛTE

The same pâté can be made *en croûte*, which means it is enveloped in a crust. It will keep longer.

Make the dough as you have done in Chapter 1 (see page 11), using the amounts given but omit the sugar and add one teaspoon salt. Butter your *terrine*, and roll ¾ of your dough to form an elongated rectangle. Put the dough in the *terrine*, so that some dough covers the inside and hangs over about an inch on all sides, and then proceed as above to make your pâté (recipe begins on page 67), putting the layers inside the pastry dough.

Roll the rest of the dough and cut a rectangle to form the top of the crust. Put it over the pâté (see illustration), and seal it by rolling the edges of the dough in the pan over the top dough. Make a hole in the center of the crust; don't go deep. Put a funnel of waxed paper in this hole, so that the steam can escape and so that later on you can remove the juice of the meat and replace it with the gelatin.

Roll the remaining dough and cut it to make flowers, leaves, any decoration you wish, for the top of your pâté. With a little bit of water, wet the top of the dough. Stick on the decorations you have cut out. (See illustration.) Take one egg, beat it up with one tablespoon of water, and brush the whole top.

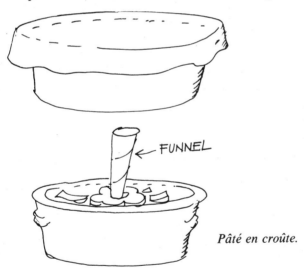

← FUNNEL

Pâté en croûte.

Bake the pâté the same way as you have done before (see page 69), until the crust is nicely browned, about 1½ hours.

When the pâté is done, let it cool for a couple of hours. Then very carefully, with a knife, remove the top crust. Be careful not to break it. If you see that it will break, then leave it as is, and add some gelatin through the funnel. If the top crust comes out easily, pour out the meat juices and replace with the gelatin, as you did before. Replace the top crust and chill until the gelatin is set. The advantage of this pâté is that it looks festive, and it will keep much longer. It is also, once refrigerated, more easily unmolded.

You can improve or change the taste of the pâté by replacing some of the ingredients. For example, you can make the pâté with pork, veal, chicken livers, but replace the chicken with ham—just plain baked ham, sliced in strips.

PORK LIVER PÂTÉ

This is a recipe that a chef in a small restaurant on the Left Bank of Paris gave my stepfather, who used to have lunch there every day. It is a lovely pâté, and only uses two kinds of meat.

WHAT DO YOU NEED?

½ **pound sliced bacon**
½ **stick butter (4 tablespoons)**
1 tablespoon flour
½ **cup hot heavy cream**
Salt and pepper
1 teaspoon each: ground nutmeg, dried tarragon, dried
  thyme
1 egg yolk
1 pound pork liver or chicken liver, ground
1 pound slab of bacon, diced fine
¼ **cup brandy**

Line the bottom of a *terrine* with three or four slices of bacon.

In a saucepan, melt the butter, and add flour. Cook the *roux* over moderately low heat for 2 or 3 minutes. Remove the pan from the heat, stir in the hot heavy cream. Add the salt, the pepper, and all the other seasonings. Cook the sauce gently on top of the stove for a couple of minutes until it is thickened, or until your wooden spoon is coated with the sauce.

Remove the pan from the heat and add the egg yolk, and stir constantly.

To this sauce, add the ground liver and the diced bacon. Add brandy, and pour the whole mixture into the *terrine*. On top of the pâté, put another two or three slices of bacon. Cover the pâté with foil, and cook as you have done before, for other pâtés, for about 1¾ hours. Remove the pâté from the oven and let it cool for at least 30 minutes. Weight it down, as you did for the five-meat pâté. Leave in the refrigerator for two or three days; slice, and serve with buttered white toast.

Now that you have done a few pâtés, experiment. Change the meats around. Add more spices. Sometimes add hard-boiled eggs or pistachio nuts. And remember that the basic recipe of a pâté is a mixture of at least two or three meats, chopped, sliced, and usually put in layers. Remember, too, that a pâté is always baked in *bain-marie,* for at least 1¾ hours. Pâtés are always served very cold, having been in the refrigerator for one or two days.

VEGETABLES AS HORS D'OEUVRES

An appetizer does not have to be a pâté or *quiche Lorraine*. It can be a plate of hors d'oeuvres: a vegetable stuffed with meat or mushrooms, smoked fish, shrimp, many other things. One of the most interesting vegetables served as an appetizer is an artichoke.

Artichokes must be boiled before they are used in any way—with the exception, maybe, of the very tiny artichoke hearts that are frozen. Artichokes are usually served cold with a vinaigrette sauce, or stuffed, or served with more elaborate sauces.

BOILED ARTICHOKES

You must always serve one artichoke per person. Choose artichokes that have no brown spots and are a light-colored green.

Remove the stems, so that when the artichokes are cooked they will stand up on the plates. Trim off the sharp tips of the artichoke leaves (about ½″) with scissors. Cook the artichokes in boiling water, with half a lemon squeezed and left in the water. The cooking time of an artichoke depends upon its size. Usually it is about 25–30 minutes. To know if an artichoke is done, just pull on one leaf; if it comes out easily, your artichoke is ready. Drain the artichokes, and put them upside down on the sink's drainboard so that all the water will seep away. Cool the artichokes and place them on a plate surrounded with parsley and lemon wedges. The diner will remove the "choke"—the spiny part above the base—after removing the outer leaves and eating their meat, then eat the base.

There are many different sauces to serve with artichokes.

VINAIGRETTE

WHAT DO YOU NEED?

2 tablespoons vinegar
½ teaspoon salt
Ground pepper
½ cup olive oil
1 chopped shallot or 1 teaspoon dried tarragon or chopped fresh parlsey

With a fork, beat together the vinegar, the salt, the pepper, and add the olive oil. When the sauce is ready, chop a shallot very fine and add to the sauce, or add one teaspoon dried tarragon or one teaspoon chopped fresh parsley.

To that sauce, to change it, you could add a teaspoon of French mustard, or one garlic clove, chopped fine.

SOUR CREAM SAUCE

Here is a nice sauce that goes well with artichokes.

WHAT DO YOU NEED?

1 cup commercial sour cream
2 teaspoons lemon juice
Salt to taste
Sugar to taste
Pepper to taste
Chives, chopped

Beat the sour cream and lemon juice together, season, sprinkle with chives, and serve very cold. It is delicious.

A nice way to serve artichokes with sour cream as hors d'oeuvre: When you have boiled the artichokes (see page 74), pull back the large leaves and remove the heart. With a spoon, scrape out the hairy part under the heart (the "choke") of the artichoke. Stuff the sour cream in the center of the artichoke, and serve it sprinkled with chives.

STUFFED ARTICHOKE BOTTOMS

This is an interesting recipe. It is done with leftover vegetables. If you have potatoes and peas and carrots or green beans cooked, from a previous dinner, you can make a stuffing for the artichoke. Boil the artichokes as before, remove the hearts and chokes and all but the outer three or four rows of leaves.

WHAT DO YOU NEED?

4 to 6 artichoke "bottoms" (prepared as above)
1½ cups cooked crab meat (may be canned)
¼ cup each, minced cooked potatoes, peas, diced carrots,
     cut string beans
1 tablespoon dried tarragon
1 tablespoon chopped fresh parsley
Salt and pepper
⅓ cup mayonnaise

If you don't want to make your own mayonnaise (see page 79), or do not have the time, use Hellmann's mayonnaise, to which you have added a teaspoon or two of lemon juice. Mix all the ingredients together, and put the mixture into the artichoke bottoms. Put the artichokes on individual plates, surrounded by parsley. You can serve the artichokes either hot or chilled.

STUFFED MUSHROOMS

The mushroom is a very versatile vegetable that you can serve as an appetizer. What you need are fairly large mushrooms that you can stuff with many different things. One interesting recipe comes from the south of France, where mushrooms are plentiful. You must serve at least three mushrooms per person. The following recipe is for five people.

WHAT DO YOU NEED?

15 large mushrooms, washed, stems removed
½ cup butter (1 stick)
4 chicken livers
3 tablespoons heavy cream
¼ cup chopped pickles
1 or 2 cloves garlic
Salt and pepper
Lemon juice
Chopped parsley

In a small frying pan, sauté the mushrooms in the butter, until they are tender. It takes 5–6 minutes. Transfer them with a slotted spoon to a dish, and let them cool. In the same pan, sauté the four chicken livers until they are done, but not overdone. Put the chicken livers in the blender with the heavy cream, the pickles, the garlic, the salt, and the pepper. Blend for a few seconds. Add the lemon juice. Correct the seasoning. Stuff the mushroom caps (upside down) with the mixture, making a little mound in each one, and sprinkle the top of the stuffing with parsley.

TOMATOES WITH AN HERB STUFFING

WHAT DO YOU NEED?

6 tomatoes
Vinaigrette sauce (see pages 74–75)
1 cup chopped fresh parsley
1 cup fresh chopped basil
2 cloves garlic
½ cup grated Parmesan cheese
Olive oil
Salt and pepper

Pour boiling water over the tomatoes. Let them stand for a few seconds; drain. Then it will be easy to remove the skins. Cut a slice from the blossom end of each tomato, and scoop up the seeds and center pulp. Make a vinaigrette dressing of oil, vinegar, salt, and pepper (see page 74), and pour over the tomatoes. Let the tomatoes marinate (soak) half an hour. Meanwhile, make stuffing. Chop the parsley and the basil; this can be done in the blender. Blend in the cloves of garlic (or finely chop and mix in). Add the cheese and enough olive oil to make a thick sauce. Add salt and pepper. Chill in the refrigerator for about one hour. When you are ready to serve, stuff tomatoes with the herb-cheese mixture and serve each on a lettuce leaf.

EGGPLANT
(BABA GHANOUG)

This is an eggplant appetizer that is nice to serve, which is eaten all over the Middle East.

WHAT DO YOU NEED?

1 medium-sized eggplant
1 clove garlic, finely chopped
1 teaspoon ground cumin
Salt and pepper
1 tablespoon lemon juice
2 tablespoons oil

In a baking dish, bake the eggplant at 350° for one hour, until it is soft. Remove from the oven, let cool, and with a fork take out the meat of the eggplant. Mash eggplant meat with a fork. Add the minced garlic. Add the cumin, the salt, the pepper, the lemon, and the oil. Mix well. It should be like a very thick paste. Refrigerate. You serve it with *pita* bread, which is a very flat bread that is also eaten in the Middle East. You can find it in many American supermarkets now.

AVOCADOS

When I first came to this country, I had never eaten an avocado pear before. I thought it was a very strange type of vegetable. Today I love it, and I very often serve it as an appetizer.

To buy avocados, choose those that are a lively green without any dark bruises on them; when they are ripe, they are soft to the touch. If you buy hard ones, let them ripen at room temperature for a few days. Refrigerate the avocados before you cut them. When you are ready to serve, cut each avocado pear in half lengthwise and remove the pit. (You can grow avocado trees, if you eat as many avocados as I do.) The basic sauce for an avocado is often a lemon and oil mixture. I improvise. I serve avocados with all sorts of different things. My basic sauce usually is a mayonnaise, to which, depending upon my mood, I add some curry powder, more lemon, some herbs, sometimes even lumpfish caviar—which is not expensive. Or I add a mustard to my mayonnaise. I also often serve the avocado stuffed with crab meat mixed with French mayonnaise for a more elaborate dinner.

MAYONNAISE

Mayonnaise is really not very difficult to make. The only thing it really requires is patience; but the result is very rewarding.

WHAT DO YOU NEED?

2 egg yolks
2 cups olive oil
Juice of 1 lemon
Salt and pepper

You can easily miss a mayonnaise. When I say "miss" a mayonnaise, I mean that your sauce—instead of being nice and thick and smooth—turns out to be a sort of liquid scrambled eggs. Here is what I do, usually, in order not to "miss" my mayonnaise: Set the bowl in which you're going to mix your mayonnaise in a bowl filled with ice. Separate the eggs. Keep the egg whites for some future use. In the iced bowl, put the two egg yolks and, with a wooden spoon and always turning slowly in the same direction, start beating the egg yolks together until they thicken. Then *drop by drop* add the oil. In the beginning, add a drop of oil, continue mixing, and add another drop of oil. As your mayonnaise will thicken you can go faster with the oil. When you have used up about a cup and a half of oil, slowly add the juice of a lemon. Then you will see that your mayonnaise will get slightly more liquid; but, as soon as you add the rest of the oil, it will thicken again. Add the salt and pepper. There you have your basic mayonnaise. If you realize, halfway through, that you have missed your mayonnaise, stop and start from the beginning. Take a clean bowl, two egg yolks, and start slowly mixing the yolks. Begin to add oil. Once you have added half a cup of oil, add—drop by drop—the mixture of the sort of liquid curdled mayonnaise that you already made. What you will end up with is twice as much mayonnaise, but it will be smooth and keep in the refrigerator for over a week if it is well covered.

To this mayonnaise you can add the following things: A teaspoon or two of mustard, chopped parsley, chopped chives, chopped tarragon, and some chervil, chopped anchovies mixed up with chopped parsley and chopped tarragon.

When you serve your avocado, fill the seed cavity with any of these mayonnaises and decorate the top with sliced hard-boiled eggs.

STUFFED HARD-BOILED EGGS
WITH TOMATO MAYONNAISE

Hard-cook six eggs. Cool them. Peel and cut in half. Remove the yolks. Pass the yolks through a fine sieve and mix them up with two slices of pimento finely chopped, some chives, some tarragon, salt and pepper. Fill the egg halves with the mixture and stick each two halves together. Put the stuffed eggs on a plate and cover them with 1¼ cups mayonnaise to which you have added half a cup of tomato purée, and maybe a little extra lemon. Sprinkle the eggs with chopped parsley. This is a delicious appetizer for a hot summer night.

Vegetables, cooked and in salads, are also a delightful appetizer. The French never throw away *"les restes,"* which are the remains of vegetables or meats served at dinner.

Vegetables for an appetizer can be beets, string beans, lima beans, potatoes, etc. The following recipe can be used for any cooked vegetable.

BEETS

Of all the vegetables, beets are the only vegetable that in France you rarely buy raw. They are always sold in the supermarket or in the market already cooked, because they take so long to cook at home. Here you often buy them in cans. This recipe is for a beet salad.

WHAT DO YOU NEED?

1-pound can whole beets
4 scallions
3 hard-boiled eggs
Vinaigrette sauce (see page 74)
Chopped fresh parsley

Slice the beets into a bowl. (The canned sliced beets are not as tender as those canned whole.) Peel scallions and slice in ¼ inch lengths; combine with beets. Add the vinaigrette. Mix well. Slice the hard-boiled eggs on top of the beets and sprinkle with parsley.

Refrigerate the salad and serve cold.

LIMA BEAN SALAD

Cooked lima beans are also delicious in salads. In the winter in France, unlike in the United States, there are very few fresh vegetables, although today, more and more, the French are getting used to frozen vegetables. When I was a child, what we mainly ate in winter were dried beans, such as lima beans and lentils and kidney beans. Lima beans and lentils in salads are delicious.

WHAT DO YOU NEED?

Canned lima beans
Vinaigrette sauce (see page 74)
Scallions, chopped
Parsley, chopped

Drain the lima beans. Mix all the ingredients together in any proportion you like and let them marinate for a couple of hours in the refrigerator. Serve cold.

HEAD CHEESE

Another salad that is very pleasant to eat is head cheese. Head cheese is a meat sausage with jelly that can be bought in supermarkets. This is the recipe I learned when I lived in Germany with my husband, while he was in the army.

WHAT DO YOU NEED?

3 medium slices of head cheese
1 small onion, chopped
Vinaigrette sauce (recipe on page 74)

Cut the sausage in small strips; they should be about ½″ wide. Chop the onion very fine. Mix the head cheese, the onion, and the vinaigrette, and let it stand for a couple of hours. Serve cold with French or Italian bread.

MELON AND PROSCIUTTO

Another excellent appetizer that requires absolutely no work is prosciutto. Prosciutto is a very tasty Italian ham which is cured and smoked and sliced very thin. It is served in Italy as an appetizer with pieces of melon. I like to serve it with pears, when they are in season; or if you can find fresh figs, they are really delicious with prosciutto. Have the prosciutto sliced paper-thin. Count three slices per person. Buy a melon; it can be a cantaloupe or a honeydew. Peel the melon. Slice it, scoop out the seeds inside, and count three slices per person. Arrange the slices on a platter, and on top of the melon put your prosciutto. Decorate the plate with sliced lime or sliced lemon. If you serve the prosciutto with fresh pears, peel the pears, leave them whole with the stems on, and surround the pears with the rolled-up prosciutto and slices of lime.

PASTA

I live in an Italian neighborhood, where spaghetti and other freshly made pasta can be bought. I often serve one of these as an appetizer; but then the main course has to be very light, as spaghetti is very filling.

To cook spaghetti, you have to remember that it needs a lot of water. Take a huge pot and fill it up with water. Add a tablespoon of salt. When the water boils, drop your spaghetti in, and with a wooden spoon turn them until they are all softened. Let the spaghetti boil for 5–8 minutes. Then pick up a strand with your wooden spoon and taste. The texture should be tender but still firm to the tooth—what the Italians call *al dente*. If the center of the spaghetti is still hard and white, then it is not yet done. Spaghetti can be served with butter and grated Parmesan cheese, or with tomato sauce, meat sauce, bacon and egg sauce, clam sauce, etc. The following recipes are basic ones that you can improvise on.

Then pick up a strand and taste.

TOMATO SAUCE

WHAT DO YOU NEED?

**2 cloves garlic, sliced
1 onion, chopped
4 tablespoons olive oil
1 small can tomato paste
3 cups hot water
2 bouillon cubes
1 tablespoon chopped fresh basil
1 tablespoon chopped fresh oregano
Salt and pepper**

In a heavy skillet, sauté the sliced garlic and chopped onion in the oil. When the onion turns a golden color and is transparent, add the tomato paste. Mix well. Be careful, because it has a tendency to splatter, and it might burn you. Add the water, the bouillon cubes, and the seasoning. Reduce the heat, and let the sauce simmer for 25–30 minutes. Taste it, and correct the seasoning. This is my basic tomato sauce.

MEAT SAUCE

Use the previous recipe, but when you fry the onions and the garlic, you add, to the oil, half a pound of chopped beef. Let the meat brown, and then proceed as you did before.

FETTUCINE ALLA CARBONARA

Fettucine is a flat, wide pasta. The kind I prefer is the green fettucine made with spinach.

WHAT DO YOU NEED?

**½ pound fettucine
4 slices bacon**

1 medium-sized onion, chopped
½ stick of butter (4 tablespoons)
2 egg yolks
½ cup freshly grated Parmesan cheese, extra cheese

Cook the fettucine as you do spaghetti, though they take less time to cook. Drain them and keep warm. In a heavy skillet, fry the bacon. Remove, and drain on a paper towel. In the same bacon fat, sauté your onion, until it is golden brown. In the pot where you have cooked your fettucine, melt the butter. Add the bacon fat and the onion. Stir in your fettucine. Add the two egg yolks, stirring continuously with a fork. Add the bacon and the Parmesan cheese. Pour the whole dish into a bowl, and serve immediately, with extra grated Parmesan cheese sprinkled on top.

SPAGHETTI WITH GREEN SAUCE

The same green sauce that you have used to stuff tomatoes (see page 77) can be used as a spaghetti sauce; the only thing you have to add is half a cup of olive oil. Heat the mixture to the boiling point and pour it over cooked spaghetti.

3 SOUPS

In France soups are always served at the beginning of the meal and often they are the meal itself. Like many people, I must be a peasant at heart; for I always feel that my dinner is missing something if I don't serve a bit of soup to start. When I was a child, the main meal was lunch. We all came back home for lunch—Papa, Maman, my brother, and I—and this would be our main meal of the day. At night we children would be served alone and the meal would consist often of a good hearty soup with fresh French bread, cheese, fruit, or a dessert. Today in France this custom is quickly changing. We eat a quick lunch and the main meal is often dinner.

Soups are easy to prepare and, with a couple of basic recipes, one can endlessly improvise. What you must remember is that the important thing in soup is the balance of flavor.

Soups may be divided into categories: There are thick soups and clear soups. Soups can be prepared with or without meat. Soups are either hot or cold. Sometimes soups are whole meals.

COOKING WITH COLETTE

To cook a soup from scratch, you need a good-sized pot, a slotted spoon, a long-pronged fork. Most of the following recipes will serve at least six people with a good appetite.

Things to remember: When you use meat, bones, or chicken to make the base of the soup, remember always to wash them well under running cold water.

Bones, chicken, and such always form a brownish scum on soup that has to be removed: It is just very unappetizing. There are many different methods of doing that, but I have found that every method requires a lot of time and takes away some of the flavor of the soup. If you wash well all the ingredients, you will find that there's very little scum and you can remove it easily with a slotted spoon.

Chicken: After washing the chicken (or the chicken parts or the chicken carcass) I always wipe the chicken with a cut lemon; the juice adds a little tangy taste to your soup.

Vegetables: Vegetables should always be washed well before cooking. Remember that vegetables cook twice as fast as meat. Therefore you should always add them to the soup halfway through the cooking.

Serving soup: Soup should be served at the boiling point if it is to be eaten hot. Nothing is more unpleasant than a tepid soup.

Cream, butter, milk, eggs: If cream or butter or eggs are to be added to the soup, the addition should be made at the last minute, after you have turned off the heat. Cream can curdle, and the soup will taste twice as good if the butter is added at the last moment.

If the recipe calls for eggs, you should always beat the eggs well with a fork. With a ladle take a spoonful of the hot soup and mix it into the eggs before adding them to the soup. If not, the eggs, like the cream, will curdle.

Garnishes: Garnish should also be put in the soup just before you are serving it or in individual soup bowls before you serve the soup, or even in a single bowl to pass around to each of your dinner guests. If you make them wait, croutons, crêpes, or anything you will use as a garnish to a clear soup will get soggy and tasteless.

CHICKEN SOUPS

WHAT DO YOU NEED?

2 pounds chicken backs and necks
Giblets from 2 chickens or 2 pounds wings
1 onion
3 cloves
1 stick celery
1 carrot
5–6 peppercorns
1 teaspoon salt
2 quarts water

Wash your chicken backs and necks and wash the giblets. Put them in a heavy pot and just cover with water. Peel the onion and stick the three cloves in it. Wash the stick of celery and scrape the carrot. Put the celery, the onion, and the carrot, the peppercorns and the salt, and the extra water in with the chicken, and bring it to a boil.

As soon as the pot starts boiling, lower the heat and, with a slotted spoon, pick off the brownish scum that appears on the top. Cook the soup for 1½ hours at medium heat. Taste. It may need more salt. It may need more pepper.

Cool the soup and then refrigerate until the fat comes to the top and you can easily take it off. Strain out the vegetables.

Now there are many ways you can use your chicken stock.

CHICKEN SOUP WITH
CRÊPES

WHAT DO YOU NEED?

6 crêpes (recipe on page 32)
1½ quarts chicken soup

Make your crêpe batter as you have done before. Use one egg less; and, instead of sugar, use a teaspoon of salt. Make your crêpes. This time brown them well on both sides. Roll up each crêpe and slice it crosswise very thinly. Serve the sliced crêpes with the very hot chicken soup. You must count one crêpe per person.

CHICKEN SOUP WITH
PÂTE À CHOUX

WHAT DO YOU NEED?

Dough for the *pâte à choux* (recipe on pages 34–36)
Salt
1 tablespoon grated Parmesan and/or Romano cheese
1½ quarts chicken soup

Make a *pâte à choux* as you have done before—add a little more salt and a tablespoon of grated Parmesan and Romano cheese; but, this time, make your balls very small—about the size of a marble. Bake the *pâte à choux* in the oven. They will take less time to cook. After 15 minutes check them. They should be golden brown. Serve them hot or cold with the very hot chicken soup.

CHICKEN SOUP WITH CROUTONS

WHAT DO YOU NEED?

1 slice white bread per person
4 slices bacon
Chicken stock

Cut each slice of bread in long strips, then cut the strips in little squares. Put the bread squares in a pan that goes in the oven and bake the bread to dry it out for 15 minutes in a 275°–300° oven. Don't let the croutons brown, just let them dry out.

In a frying pan, sauté the bacon until it is crisp. Eat it—it's very good. Then take the croutons and sauté them in the bacon fat. Serve them piping hot with the soup. What I sometimes do while they are sautéing in the bacon fat is to add a teaspoon or two of dried tarragon or to sprinkle them with grated Parmesan cheese. This is also very tasty.

You can also give the croutons a garlic taste. When you are ready to sauté the croutons, don't use bacon fat; this time, use some olive oil and crush a piece of garlic and sauté it in the oil first.

CHICKEN SOUP WITH VEGETABLES

This time, the vegetables are going to be served in the soup. Proceed as for the recipe for chicken soup (page 88); but this time have one carrot (medium size) per person, one turnip (small) per person, two or three potatoes, peeled and diced, and two or three pieces of celery, cut in 1″ pieces, ready. Do not add them at the beginning of the cooking time.

Proceed as before. Halfway through cooking, add the vegetables. The most important thing you have to remember is that the vegetables should not be overdone. To know if they are ready, take a fork and pierce the carrot. If the carrot is done, they are all done. Remove the meat with a slotted spoon, the giblets and the backs or carcass, if you have used that for your chicken soup. Cut the giblets in small pieces. Cut the meat on the chicken in small pieces. Return all the meat to the soup. Serve very hot.

Now that you have experimented with chicken stock, you can find other ways to serve this clear *bouillon*—that's the French word for a clear meat broth (it means something boiled). You can add, for example, a little Italian pasta. Some good choices are shaped like little shells or stars; one kind—called *orzo*—is as small as barley and good in soup. Follow the directions on the box. It is very simple. You can serve the soup with a poached egg and chopped parsley. Sprinkle some Parmesan or Romano cheese on it. Or use your imagination and see what you get.

BEEF SOUPS

I like to make a lot of beef soup, for you can use it endlessly. It can be easily frozen or kept at least for a week in the refrigerator. And it is a very good base for many, many tasty soups.

BASIC BEEF SOUP

WHAT DO YOU NEED?

2 pounds short ribs of beef or beef shanks
1 pound chicken giblets
1–2 beef bones
1 carrot
1 celery stick
1 bay leaf
1 onion, stuck with several cloves
Salt and pepper
3 quarts cold water

Wash the shanks or the short ribs under cold running water and put them in a heavy pot. Add the chicken giblets; the bones, washed and clean; the carrot, scraped; the celery; the bay leaf; the onion with the cloves; the pepper and the salt. Cover with three quarts of water—cold water. When the soup is about to boil start skimming the top. Do it a couple of times until the bouillon is nearly clear. Then, on medium heat, let the soup cook for at least an hour.

Strain the bouillon through a thin sieve. When I don't have a very fine sieve, what I often use are two layers of paper towels inside my colander; and I find that this helps a lot to strain out all the little pieces of bones and skin that are in the soup. Refrigerate the cooled soup for a couple of hours so that the fat will solidify on top and you can very easily remove it with a spoon.

BEEF SOUP WITH MARROW BALLS

You can use any of the garnishes that you have used for the chicken soup for the beef broth. If it is going to be a clear bouillon, sometimes I add a teaspoon of soy sauce, to give it color. Marrow is a marvelous combination with a beef broth.

WHAT DO YOU NEED?

1½ tablespoons beef marrow (5–6 bones)
3 tablespoons dried bread crumbs
1½ teaspoons finely chopped fresh parsley
1 teaspoon grated lemon rind
Salt and pepper
1 unbeaten egg white
A pinch of nutmeg (optional)

Go to the butcher and ask him for marrow bones. Sometimes you can find them in the supermarket. With a sharp knife remove the marrow from the bones. Don't worry if it crumbles into little pieces. In a bowl, combine the bread crumbs, the marrow, the chopped parsley, the grated lemon rind, the salt, and the other seasonings. Then add the egg white—egg white is necessary to moisten the mixture—and, with a fork, mix it well. Shape it into small balls, like marbles. Heat the soup to the boiling point and drop the "marbles" into the soup. When you drop them they will sink to the bottom of the pot, and you will know that they are done when they start to float; because marrow is heavy when it is raw, but light as air when it is cooked.

To make your soup even more elegant and more tasty, add a tablespoon of chopped shallots. Serve the soup with slices of toast cut in triangles.

You can follow the recipe above but replace the marrow bones with the meat cooked in the soup. Put the meat in the blender, or chop it up and follow the same recipe. Make your spices a little bit heavier. Maybe add a little bit of cayenne pepper, because the beef—having cooked for an hour—is less tasty than the marrow.

Sometimes I have no time to cook a soup and prepare it in advance. Here is a little secret I share with you, but don't tell your guests what you are serving. For six people take two cans of Campbell's Beef Consommé; add two cans of water. Add a little bit more pepper, and a tablespoon of sherry. Make your marrow balls and serve the soup sprinkled with chopped parsley. The soup is nearly as good as if you had made your own. Twice as quick and not very expensive.

POT-AU-FEU

Pot-au-feu is a traditional French soup. At least once a week, once a month, in every family in the winter, there was a *pot-au-feu*. It is a meal in itself and really a family soup. It is a soup that can be kept and reheated and it will taste even better the next day. Today this soup, which used to be a cheap meal, is expensive to make because meat is expensive; and therefore it has become a soup that you serve on a special occasion.

The proportions that follow are really for at least ten people. Therefore, if you make this soup, you can be sure that you will have it for more than one meal. It can easily be frozen.

WHAT DO YOU NEED?

3 pounds beef round steak or chuck in 1 piece
1½ pounds short ribs of beef

1 pound beef bones
5 quarts cold water
1 onion stuck with several cloves
Salt
5–6 peppercorns

Start the soup as in the previous recipe (on page 92). Cook it for an hour. Once your basic soup is made, cook the vegetables.

WHAT DO YOU NEED?

6 turnips
6 medium-sized carrots
2 leeks
5 parsnips
1 bay leaf
1 clove of garlic
½ small cabbage

Cut bases off leeks and peel off outer layers; wash well. Scrub and wash all other vegetables. Scrape the turnips and parsnips and cut in quarters. Scrape the carrots and cut in two. Crush the garlic and add along with the bay leaf and all the previous vegetables to the soup. The cabbage, which is a strong vegetable, has to be cooked separately. In a pot, cover the cabbage with boiling water and cook it for 8–10 minutes. When the soup is ready and the vegetables are cooked, drain the cabbage and add it to the soup. You can serve the soup separately with the vegetables on a side dish, or everything together. What is marvelous to serve with this soup is *aioli* with French bread.

AIOLI

What is *aioli? Aioli* is a garlic mayonnaise. It is very strong. It comes from the south of France where garlic is eaten a lot. It is a marvelous sauce to eat spread on hot French bread with a *pot-au-feu.* It is good with the meat and it is good with the soup.

AIOLI!

It is very strong.

1 cup mayonnaise (recipe on page 79)
4–6 garlic cloves
Lemon juice

Peel the garlic cloves and in a mortar pound the garlic with a pestle. When the garlic is like a paste, add it to the mayonnaise that you have done before. Add lemon juice, and correct the seasoning. You can also, if you don't have a mortar and a pestle, put the peeled garlic in a blender and blend it with some of the mayonnaise; then mix with the rest of the mayonnaise. If I am in a hurry, I use a garlic press to crush the garlic. The idea is to have a strong, garlicky mayonnaise. When you serve the soup, have some French or Italian bread or even white toast, and serve the *aioli* at the same time that you serve your very, very hot soup. With it serve a nice salad and a dessert, and you have a fabulous meal.

VEGETABLE SOUPS

You can make soups without any meat or poultry, just with vegetables; and they can be delicious. One of my favorite winter or summer vegetable soups is a watercress soup. In America, watercress is plentiful and always fresh and beautiful. When you buy watercress, be sure that the leaves are crisp, dark green, and not wilted.

WATERCRESS SOUP

WHAT DO YOU NEED?

4 potatoes, peeled and quartered
3 cups sliced leeks or 1½ cups sliced scallions or 2 cups chopped yellow onions
2 quarts water
1 bunch watercress
2 tablespoons butter, plus extra butter or cream
1 tablespoon salt
Pepper to taste

Put the potatoes and the leeks or onions to boil in the water for 30–35 minutes, or until the potatoes fall apart. Meanwhile wash the watercress. Keep three or four branches of watercress for decorating the soup. In a small saucepan, melt the butter and sauté the watercress for a few minutes. Add salt and pepper. In the blender, pour the water and the potatoes and onions and blend well. You might have to do it in two or three batches, because most blenders will not hold two quarts of water. Put most of the soup back in the pot, but keep one cup of soup in the blender. Add the watercress and blend well. Add the soup and watercress to the large pot of soup. Correct the seasoning. Now if you want to make the soup a little bit richer, add at the last minute ½ cup heavy cream or two to three tablespoons butter. Serve the soup very hot and drop in each bowl one or two leaves of whole watercress.

BROCCOLI SOUP

Follow the same recipe as above but use broccoli instead of watercress. Use half a bunch of broccoli; wash it well and cut it into small pieces; boil in water for 5–6 minutes. Drain the broccoli and then proceed as in the watercress soup. We don't have broccoli in France, and it is a vegetable that I adore. So do my children. Try the broccoli soup—you will see.

I have also made soup with string beans by cooking the string beans first and following the recipe for the watercress soup. All these vegetable soups can also be served cold. If you serve them cold, you can make them in advance and refrigerate them for a couple of hours and, at the last minute, add half a cup of heavy cream. Serve the soup with little triangles of toasted white bread or with hot French or Italian bread.

POTATO AND LEEK SOUP

Soupe aux poireaux et pommes de terre (leek and potato soup) is traditional in France. When you enter a French apartment house and go past the *concierge* (she's the woman who keeps the house—she's more than a "super"), you always smell in the staircase the subtle aroma of potato and leek. Leeks are hard to find in the United States, and they are expensive. But if you live in a town where leeks are available, try this soup once. It is a fantastic soup.

WHAT DO YOU NEED?

4 potatoes
1½ pounds leeks
1 tablespoon salt
Pepper to taste
2 quarts chicken soup (recipe on page 88)
½ cup heavy cream
2 tablespoons butter

Go past the concierge.

Peel and dice the potatoes. Peel and chop the leeks. Leeks look like big, overgrown scallions. To peel leeks, you have to cut off the base and take off the outer layer. Then wash the leeks very well; they are often full of sand. Put the leeks and the potatoes, the salt and the pepper, in a big saucepan. Add the chicken stock. Cook until the potatoes are tender. This time be careful; don't overcook the potatoes. They have to stay whole. Taste the soup and correct the seasoning. When you are ready to serve, taste the soup again; and add the heavy cream and the butter. Turn off the heat immediately and serve piping hot; you will find yourself in Paris.

CREAM SOUPS

You learned in Chapter 1 (page 29) how to make a *roux.* Now you can use a *roux* to make a cream soup. You can make cream of mushroom or cream of celery soup; there is a basic recipe also for making a bisque. A bisque is a cream soup that has tomato in it and to which you add shrimp or any shellfish.

CREAM OF MUSHROOM

WHAT DO YOU NEED?

**10–12 mushrooms
4 tablespoons butter
1 teaspoon brandy
Salt and pepper
2 tablespoons flour
5 cups chicken stock, heated
1 cup heavy cream
2 teaspoons chopped parsley**

Wash your mushrooms carefully. Keep two mushrooms to decorate your soup. Chop the rest of the mushrooms, including the stems. In a frying pan, melt two tablespoons butter. Sauté your mushrooms. Add the brandy and salt and pepper to taste. Let the mushrooms cool. Meanwhile, using the other two tablespoons of butter and the flour, make your *roux* (see page 29). When it is well cooked, stir in the hot chicken stock. For the chicken consommé, you may use chicken consommé in cans (diluted) or 1 bouillon cube for each cup of boiling water. When your soup is smooth, add more salt and pepper. Add the mushrooms and the butter in which they have cooked. Mix well. Taste it and correct the seasoning. When you are ready to serve, heat the soup again if necessary and add the heavy cream. Once you have added the heavy cream, don't boil the soup: serve it. When you serve the soup, cut the two mushrooms you have saved into slices and put 2–3 slices in each soup bowl. Sprinkle with parsley.

CREAM OF CELERY

Follow the recipe above.
When I make a celery soup, I use celeriac, which is a root of

celery. You need one celeriac. Peel and quarter the celeriac; cook it in boiling water. The root is done when it feels tender when you prick it with a fork. Drain it. Make the *roux,* and stir in the chicken broth to make the basic soup as for cream of mushroom. Put the celeriac in the blender and add one cup of the creamed soup that you have made as a base. Blend. Pour the celeriac back in the saucepan with the rest of the soup, add the cream, a teaspoon of brandy, and correct the seasoning with salt and pepper as needed. A nice garnish with this soup is croutons and some chopped parsley.

BISQUE

The basic recipe for a bisque is the same if you use shrimp or crab or pieces of lobster.

BISQUE MADE WITH SHRIMPS

WHAT DO YOU NEED?

1 pound shrimps
4 tablespoons butter
2 shallots, chopped
2 teaspoons brandy
2 tablespoons flour
5 cups chicken consommé
1 tablespoon tomato paste
1 bay leaf
1 pinch cayenne pepper
Salt and pepper to taste
1 cup heavy cream
Chopped fresh parsley

Clean the shrimps as you have learned to do in Chapter 2 (pages 60–61). In a frying pan, melt two tablespoons of butter and sauté the chopped shallots. Cut the shrimps in small pieces and sauté them until they turn pink. Make the *roux* and cream soup as you have done above with 2 tablespoons butter, the flour, and the consommé (recipe for *roux* on page 29). Add the tomato paste to the soup. Keep two or three pieces of shrimp per person. Put the rest in the blender. Add a cup of soup and blend. Pour the shrimp from the blender into the remaining soup. Add the bay leaf and the shallots with the butter they have cooked in to the soup. Add the brandy, a pinch of cayenne, salt and pepper, taste, correct the seasoning, and heat it up. When the soup is hot, add the heavy cream. Do not boil. Cut the remaining shrimps in tiny pieces and put them in the soup. Sprinkle with parsley and serve. Serve this soup with French bread or Italian bread or white toast.

CLAM CHOWDER

This is a recipe I make that my children love and that is very quick to do.

WHAT DO YOU NEED?

4 tablespoons butter
1 shallot, chopped
1 medium onion, chopped
1 garlic clove, finely chopped
⅓ cup chopped celery
1½ quarts fresh clams or 2 7-ounce cans chopped clams
2 8-ounce bottles clam juice
Salt and pepper to taste
½ cup heavy cream
Chopped parsley

In a skillet, melt the butter. Add the onions and the shallots and cook gently. When the onions are soft and transparent, add the garlic, and the celery. Cook until the celery is done. Clean and wash the clams in running cold water. In a heavy pot put the wet clams and steam them until they are open. Let them cool. Shell the clams and chop them fine. Add the clams to the frying pan with the onion, celery, and garlic and sauté the clams for a few minutes. Strain the juice of the clams through a fine sieve, return to the pot and add the clams, the celery, garlic, and onions along with the two bottles of clam juice. Taste the soup. It might need salt and pepper. If it is too strong add two cups of boiling water. When the soup is very hot, just before you serve it, add the cream. When you serve, put in each bowl a teaspoon of chopped parsley.

DRIED BEAN SOUPS

In the winter I like to make soups with lentils or split peas or black beans. On a cold night, it is warming to eat a lentil soup with frankfurters or a split pea soup. It is a hearty meal.

LENTIL SOUP

WHAT DO YOU NEED?

**1 pound lentils
8 cups water
1 medium onion
2 beef bones
Salt and pepper
3 slices bacon
3 cloves garlic, chopped
5 frankfurters, sliced thin**

In a saucepan, cover the lentils with water. There should be about 2–3 inches of water above the lentils. Peel the onion and add it to the pot. Wash the beef bones carefully. Add them to the pot. Add salt and pepper and cook on medium heat. When the soup starts to boil, skim the top. The lentils should cook for about ¾–1 hour. Meanwhile, in a frying pan, sauté the bacon. When the bacon is cooked, drain it on a paper towel. To the bacon fat, add the chopped garlic. Sauté the garlic until it is just lightly brown. Add the garlic and three tablespoons bacon fat to the soup. Correct the seasoning. Crumble the bacon and add it to the soup.

Slice the frankfurters very thin and add them to the soup. When the frankfurters are hot, your soup is ready.

Lentil soup is even tastier if you do it one day in advance and let it stand. The second day it is even better.

PEA SOUP

WHAT DO YOU NEED?

8 cups water
1 pound split peas
1 onion, chopped
1 smoked pork hock or 1 ham bone with some meat
Garlic clove, crushed (optional)
Salt and pepper
½ cup heavy cream
1 tablespoon butter

In a heavy pot, put the split peas and, as for the lentils, cover them with 2–3 inches of water. Peel and add the onion. Add the smoked pork hock or ham bone, and cook the soup on medium heat for about an hour, until the peas have softened completely and the whole soup looks like a cream. You can add a crushed garlic clove. Taste the soup. Correct the seasoning, adding salt and pepper if needed. Just before serving, add the heavy cream and one tablespoon of butter. Serve this soup with croutons sautéed in bacon fat (recipe on pages 89–90).

COLD SOUPS

In the summer when the weather is very hot, you cannot serve a hot soup. Then, cold soups are delightful at the beginning of the meal. A cold soup could be the watercress soup that you have already made, served cold.

You can also serve cold the potato and leek soup (page 97); purée the soup in the blender and add an extra ¼ cup heavy cream. Serve it with chopped parsley, chopped mint, or even a leaf of basil, or add a spoon of sour cream to each bowl instead of adding the extra cream.

GAZPACHO

Another lovely cold soup is a Spanish gazpacho. Gazpacho is a soup made out of tomatoes and onions and olive oil and served with raw green pepper, onions, and tomatoes. A Spanish friend of mine told me that each province in Spain or each South American country has a different recipe for gazpacho. But here is mine, which is really a combination of different recipes.

WHAT DO YOU NEED?

1 garlic clove
1 onion, chopped
5 ripe tomatoes, peeled and cored
1 cup beef stock
3 tablespoons oil
1 tablespoon vinegar
1 tablespoon chopped fresh parsley
Dash of paprika
½ avocado, peeled and sliced

What is interesting about this soup is that it needs no cooking. In a blender put all these ingredients. Blend well for two minutes and chill it in the refrigerator. Gazpacho is always served with chopped raw vegetables:

WHAT DO YOU NEED?

1 cup chopped tomatoes
1 cup chopped onion
1 cup chopped green pepper
1 cup croutons

You serve the soup and in the center of the table you put the bowls of vegetables. Each guest will take some tomato, some onion, some green pepper, and some croutons, and add them to the bowl of soup.

ALAN'S SOUP

Here is another summer soup served cold that we made in East Hampton. A friend of mine, Alan Buschbaum, wanted to make a soup, so he took all the fresh vegetables I had in the refrigerator, and this is what he made.

WHAT DO YOU NEED?

1 pound string beans
2 carrots, scraped
3 sticks celery, washed
1 onion, chopped
Salt and pepper
1 clove garlic
1 pound spinach, washed
5 cups chicken stock
1 tablespoon butter

Wash the string beans and cut them in 1″ pieces. In a heavy pot, put the string beans, the carrots cut in pieces, the celery cut in pieces, the onion, and salt and pepper. Cover with water and cook until the carrots are done. Drain the vegetables; put them in the blender. Add a clove of garlic and the spinach. Add to the blender two cups of the chicken bouillon. You can either make it from scratch (recipe on page 88) or use one bouillon cube per cup of boiling water. Blend well. Return the blended soup to the saucepan with the rest of the bouillon. Correct the seasoning, adding salt and pepper. Put a tablespoon of butter in; and, when the butter is melted, cover the soup and refrigerate it for a couple of hours. Serve it with a leaf or two of parsley sprinkled on top of the soup. It is really delicious.

CUCUMBER SOUP

Here is another good cold soup, a recipe for a cucumber soup with yogurt that needs no cooking.

WHAT DO YOU NEED?

4 cups plain yogurt
⅓ cup heavy cream
3 tablespoons chopped fresh mint, extra mint leaves
Juice of 2 lemons
2 cups chicken consommé
1 medium cucumber, peeled and chopped

In a bowl combine the yogurt, the heavy cream, the mint, the juice, and the chicken consommé. You can use canned soup or chicken bouillon cubes. Chop the cucumber, put it in the blender with one cup of the yogurt-consommé mixture. Blend well, add the mixture to the yogurt, and refrigerate. Serve cold, with a leaf of mint in each bowl.

This last recipe is the famous French onion soup *au gratin.* This soup has to be served on a very cold winter night, or late at night when you have been out all day and you come home cold and you want some very warm soup that really fills you up.

ONION SOUP

SOUPE À L'OIGNON AU GRATIN

WHAT DO YOU NEED?

¼ cup butter (4 tablespoons)
4 medium-sized onions
1 tablespoon flour

6 cups beef stock (recipe on page 91 or use canned consommé or bouillon cubes)
1 teaspoon salt
Pepper to taste
6 tablespoons grated Parmesan cheese
6 tablespoons grated Swiss cheese
6 slices French bread, toasted
6 slices Gruyere or other Swiss cheese
6 small pieces butter

In a large saucepan, melt the butter. Cut the onions in very thin slices and sauté them in the butter for at least 15–20 minutes over a low flame until they are golden color. Sprinkle the onions with the flour and stir well until all the flour is incorporated into the butter on the onions. Add the beef stock, about a teaspoon of salt, and pepper to taste. Warm six ovenproof soup bowls. Divide the soup among the six soup bowls. Add one tablespoon of each grated cheese to each soup bowl. Float a slice of toasted French bread on top of each portion. Add, on top of the bread, a slice of Gruyere or Swiss cheese cut into 2 or 3 pieces. Put a little piece of butter on top of each pile of cheese. Put the bowls in the oven at 400° until the cheese is melted and is golden brown. Serve immediately.

4 VEGETABLES

Most children do not like vegetables. I really don't know why. My son, for example, only likes cauliflower and broccoli. Any other vegetable, he says, is "gross." And my youngest daughter will eat string beans and nothing else. Myself, I remember, as a child, I disliked vegetables. The one I disliked the most was spinach. I always thought that my mother and our nurse, whom we called Mademoiselle, must have seen a lot of Popeye cartoons; for always we were served spinach at least two or three times a week, and Mademoiselle would stand in front of me and say, "Eat, it's good for you! It makes you strong!" And I used to look at this green mush served on my plate and wonder, What was in it? What mysterious thing was in spinach that would make me strong? And, after being coaxed, and menaced, and cajoled, I would finally eat it and find out that nothing special did happen to me after dinner. But vegetables do not have to be bad or boring. Vegetables, well prepared, undercooked, crisp, and well seasoned, can be delightful—especially in the summer, when they are so plentiful. Nothing is more marvelous than a spinach salad, or string beans done with garlic and parsley, or fresh corn on the cob.

Eat, it's good for you! It makes you strong!

You must remember that, if you have any leftover vegetables, they can be served in a salad, or a vinaigrette, the following day. The French never throw away any vegetables. They always serve them as a salad or an appetizer or at lunch time the next day.

SPINACH

Spinach in supermarkets is often sold in bags, already washed. When you buy spinach this way, you have to be careful that there is no darkness in the bag, that there is no moisture—because that will mean the spinach leaves are withered or nearly spoiled and that they will not keep for any period of time in your refrigerator. If you buy fresh spinach loose, you have to count a little bit more per person, because the stems are left on the spinach leaves. When you choose spinach, the leaves should be dark green, bright in color, and crisp. The leaves should be young; if it's overgrown spinach, it is usually tasteless.

When you buy spinach, even if you buy it in a bag, it should be washed under cold running water; because often the spinach leaves have sand. One thing you always have to remember is that spinach needs no water to cook. It gives off a lot of water when it cooks; and, if you added any water, the leaves would lose all their taste. Wash the spinach well, drain it in a colander, and put it in a pot and cook it. Just watch when you are cooking, for it will cook very fast; and you will see that, even then, you will have at least a cup of liquid or half a cup of liquid per pound of spinach.

On page 54, you learned to make a spinach soufflé; here is another good spinach dish.

BOILED SPINACH WITH GARLIC

WHAT DO YOU NEED?

2 pounds spinach
Salt and pepper to taste
2 tablespoons olive oil
1 clove garlic, chopped

Wash your spinach well; drain it; put in a heavy saucepan. Add the salt and pepper. Cook the spinach over moderate heat, and keep stirring so the leaves do not burn on one side. Spinach should cook very quickly, 5–6 minutes, no more. Drain the spinach. In the saucepan, heat the olive oil, a little more salt and pepper, and the chopped garlic. Sauté the garlic for 1 or 2 minutes. Add the spinach, turn it in the oil.

A very pleasant way to serve spinach for lunch or for a light dinner—if you have, for example, a substantial soup to start—is spinach with poached eggs.

SPINACH WITH POACHED EGGS

Cook the spinach as before. Poach one egg per person (see pages 63–64). Place each poached egg on a serving of spinach and sprinkle the egg with Parmesan cheese. Serve with white toast.

STRING BEANS

How to buy string beans: In America you can get fresh string beans all year round. The smaller or thinner the string beans, the better. To know if a string bean is really fresh, take one and break it in two. If it's crisp, and if the inside looks wet and bright, the string bean is fresh. The beans should be a nice, light-green color. You should use, for six people, about three pounds of string beans. You have to snip or break off the ends of each string bean before you cook them. Sometimes the bean has a string (it gives the bean its name) that goes along the sides. When you break each end, you will find out by pulling carefully if there is any string on the side—it will pull off with the top. Never overcook string beans; they should be crunchy, and they should cook in a lot of water, quickly, and be drained immediately. Never leave the string beans in boiling water. They will very quickly become like mashed vegetables.

FRENCH STRING BEANS

WHAT DO YOU NEED?

3 pounds string beans
2 teaspoons salt
2 tablespoons butter
2 cloves garlic
1 tablespoon chopped fresh parsley

In a heavy saucepan, cover your string beans with water. Add the salt. Boil for about 15 minutes, or until when pierced with a fork the beans seem tender. Drain the string beans. In the saucepan, melt the butter. Add the garlic, chopped, and the parsley; cook gently. It should then fill your kitchen with a wonderful aroma. When the garlic is a golden light-brown color, return your string beans to the pot and sauté them for a few minutes, turning with a wooden spoon continuously. Serve piping hot.

An even more elegant way to serve string beans is to add toasted or grilled slivered almonds. You can buy the almonds in a supermarket, already blanched and slivered, and what you have to do is put them in a roasting pan, set your oven at 350°, and heat them in the oven for 10 minutes. Stir the almonds frequently, so they do not burn, until they get a sort of golden-brown color. Then sprinkle the nuts at the last moment on top of your string beans. It should make a lovely looking vegetable.

BROCCOLI

I had never seen broccoli before I came to the United States. In France, we have brussels sprouts; we have string beans; we have every other vegetable except broccoli. And, in the beginning, I did not know how to cook broccoli; but it is one of my children's favorite vegetables. They got interested in broccoli, they experimented with different recipes, and this is what they came up with.

BROCCOLI SAUTÉ

You buy a bunch of broccoli—one bunch will serve four to six people. Cut off the heavy ends. Keep the flower and about two inches of the stem. Wash well and drain. Put the broccoli in a heavy saucepan and cover with water. Add a teaspoon of salt, and let the stalks boil until, when pierced with a fork, they are tender, about 10 minutes. Don't overcook them. Drain immediately. Never leave any vegetable in water; it will lose all its taste.

Once your broccoli is cooked, there are many ways to serve it. You can proceed as for the sautéed spinach, with the garlic and oil (see page 110). Or you can cook broccoli the Chinese way.

CHINESE BROCCOLI

WHAT DO YOU NEED?

1 bunch broccoli
2 tablespoons oil
1 clove garlic, crushed
2 tablespoons soy sauce
¼ teaspoon powdered ginger

Undercook your broccoli, which means barely cook the stalks in water for 10 minutes, no longer. Drain well. In a heavy skillet, heat your oil. Sauté the crushed garlic. When the oil is very hot, add quickly your broccoli, and sauté for a few minutes. Add the soy sauce and the ginger, and serve immediately. The sautéing of the broccoli should only take about 2 or 3 minutes, no more.

BROCCOLI WITH HOLLANDAISE

Another way to serve broccoli is with a hollandaise sauce.

WHAT DO YOU NEED?

1 bunch broccoli
2 sticks butter (½ pound)
4 egg yolks
1½ tablespoons water or tarragon vinegar
Salt and lemon juice to taste

Boil your broccoli as in the preceding recipe. Don't overcook. Make a hollandaise sauce. Now a hollandaise sauce is not very easy to make. I have often failed, and have found out why—so don't worry. Do everything carefully and you will succeed.

VEGETABLES **113**

To make a hollandaise sauce, you need a double boiler. Fill the bottom half full of water and heat until it is simmering. Divide your butter in six equal pieces. In the top of the double boiler, over the simmering water, put your egg yolks with the 1½ teaspoons of water or vinegar and, with a whisk, beat rapidly and continuously until the yolks thicken. Then add one piece of butter, and beat continuously until the first piece of butter has been absorbed by the eggs. You must beat the eggs *all* the time. Add a second piece of butter, and continue to beat. Continue in this way until you have used all the butter. Add the salt and lemon juice to taste. If you see that the sauce shows signs of curdling, which means that your egg yolks are turning into scrambled eggs, add a few drops of water and continue to beat. Or you can pour the egg mixture slowly into another bowl with one tablespoon of lemon juice in it, beating all the time; and you might save your sauce. Once your sauce is done, you must be careful not to cook it any longer. To keep hollandaise warm, you can keep it in a shallow pan of warm water until you are ready to use it. This sauce can be refrigerated for a couple of days. To reheat hollandaise, put the bowl in a pan of hot water and beat continuously until sauce is warm.

This sauce is also very good with asparagus or boiled artichokes. When I serve it with boiled artichokes, I add four or five tablespoons of whipped heavy cream to my hollandaise, and it makes the sauce lighter to eat.

CAULIFLOWER

Cauliflower is a marvelous vegetable, because it looks so beautiful when it is served whole. When you buy cauliflower, it should have no brown spots, and the green leaves at the bottom of the cauliflower should be crisp. You will know then that your cauliflower is fresh. Rinse the cauliflower under cold water. Cut the heavy stem away. If you are going to serve it whole, boil it whole. If you are going to serve it with a white sauce, or gratinée, then you can cut the little florets apart first or separate them into small pieces after you have boiled it.

BOILED CAULIFLOWER
WITH BUTTER AND PARSLEY

Put your whole cauliflower in a heavy saucepan. Add three cups of water, one teaspoon of salt, and boil the cauliflower. You will know it is done when you pierce it with a fork and the fork goes in easily. Don't overcook the cauliflower. Drain it. Put it on a serving dish. In a saucepan melt two tablespoons of butter; mix in a teaspoon of lemon juice, some salt and pepper. Pour the butter over the cauliflower, and sprinkle with chopped parsley.

CAULIFLOWER WITH A
BÉCHAMEL SAUCE AU GRATIN

WHAT DO YOU NEED?

1 cauliflower
1 tablespoon chopped onion
2 tablespoons butter
2 tablespoons flour
3 cups hot milk
Salt and pepper
A pinch ground nutmeg
3 tablespoons grated Swiss cheese
2 or 3 pats butter
Chopped parsley

In a heavy saucepan, cook the cauliflower, following the directions above. When the cauliflower is cooked, drain it and cool it. Meanwhile, make a béchamel sauce. A béchamel sauce follows the same principle as the sauce you made with a *roux* for a soufflé (see page 29). In a saucepan, sauté the onion in two tablespoons of butter. Add the flour and mix well. Cook this *roux* slowly, stirring constantly, until it just starts to get golden colored. Gradually add the hot milk, mixing continuously with a wire whisk, until the sauce is very thick and smooth. Add salt and pepper to taste, and a pinch of nutmeg.

In a dish that can go in the oven, separate the florets of the cauliflower. Spread them in the dish. Pour the white sauce—béchamel—over the cauliflower. On top of the white sauce, sprinkle the grated Swiss cheese. Add a couple of pats of butter, and put the dish under the broiler, or put it in the oven at 375°, until it is golden brown. When you are ready to serve, sprinkle a little bit of chopped parsley on top; and you have a delicious vegetable dish.

CARROTS

Carrots are usually sold in packages. Very thick carrots are good in soup; but carrots that you are going to serve as a vegetable should be slender ones. Wash the carrots carefully and scrape them with a knife, or peel them with a potato peeler.

CARROTS SAUTÉED IN BUTTER

Count one carrot per person, if they are big, or two small ones.

WHAT DO YOU NEED?

12 small carrots
1 teaspoon salt
2 tablespoons butter
1 tablespoon sugar
Lemon juice (optional)
Chopped parsley

Wash and scrape or peel your carrots. Set them in a saucepan, and cover them with water. Add a teaspoon of salt. Cook the carrots until they are tender, but not quite done; you test them with the point of a paring knife or with a fork. Drain. Cut the carrots in 1″ pieces. In a heavy saucepan, melt the butter. Add your carrots, and the sugar, and cook for 3 or 4 minutes, until the carrots are all coated with the butter. Then put the heat quite high, so that the sugar will burn slightly, and will give a sort of caramel taste to your carrots. Do that for a minute or two. Sometimes I add a teaspoon of lemon juice; and, when I serve the carrots, I sprinkle them with parsley, so the orange color and the green of the parsley make each other brighter.

BRUSSELS SPROUTS

Brussels sprouts are another pleasant vegetable. Brussels sprouts are usually sold by the quart, and they look like little cabbages. When you buy them, the outer leaves should not be yellow. They should be green. You cut off the bottoms of the stalks and pull off any wilted leaves.

BRUSSELS SPROUTS WITH BACON OR LEMON BUTTER

WHAT DO YOU NEED?

1 quart brussels sprouts
3 slices bacon
Salt and pepper
Chopped parsley

Wash the brussels sprouts and trim as described above. Simmer the sprouts in salted water to cover for about 20 minutes, or until they are tender when pierced with a knife. Drain well. In a heavy saucepan, heat the bacon; cook it until it is nice and crisp. Remove the bacon and drain on paper towels. In the bacon fat, sauté the brussels sprouts for a few minutes. Taste the seasoning, correct, and add pepper. When you are ready to serve, crumble the bacon over the brussels sprouts and add a little bit of chopped parsley. You can do without the bacon. If you do not use bacon, heat half a stick of butter until it is nearly brown. Add the grated rind of one lemon, and about a teaspoon of lemon juice. Pour the lemon butter over the brussels sprouts, add chopped parsley.

CELERY

Celery is very rarely served as a vegetable in the United States, although often it is used as an appetizer, cut in small pieces and served nice and crisp and ice-cold. But celery *au gratin* is a very good vegetable.

CELERY AU GRATIN

WHAT DO YOU NEED?

1 large head celery
¾ stick butter (6 tablespoons)
Béchamel sauce (recipe on page 115)
¾ cup grated Swiss cheese
Salt and pepper

Take a large head of celery and, after removing the root end and the leaves, cut it crosswise in very thin slices. In a heavy saucepan, melt all but one pat of the butter. Add the celery, and cook it, stirring continuously with a fork, until it is just tender. Pour the celery into a baking dish and cover with the béchamel sauce, made following the recipe used for cauliflower (page 115). Add the grated Swiss cheese, some salt and fresh ground pepper, a pat of butter in little pieces. Bake the dish in a hot oven, 375°, until it is golden brown. Serve piping hot.

ASPARAGUS

Asparagus is plentiful in the spring. Asparagus comes in different sizes. Some French asparagus can be as thick as an inch in diameter. Some asparagus is white, and some is green. But all asparagus is very, very tasty.

Asparagus, when you buy it, should be very firm. The stalks have to be washed very carefully, because they are often full of sand. What I often do is to let them soak in water with a tablespoon of vinegar and then rinse them again. Asparagus, like any other vegetable, should be cooked until just done. Overcooked asparagus is difficult to eat; if you pick up the stalks with your fingers, they may collapse!

BOILED ASPARAGUS

Wash the asparagus carefully. Cut off the tough bottom part (usually an inch or two). Place the stalks carefully in a heavy skillet and cover with water halfway. Add a teaspoon of salt, and simmer the asparagus. The stalks are tender when they can be pricked easily with a fork. Drain them immediately. You have to be careful, because the stalks can break easily; you should lift them up carefully with two spatulas and put them in a hot serving dish.

You can serve the asparagus with a vinaigrette sauce (see page 74) or with a hollandaise sauce (see pages 113–114) or with a melted butter sauce. For the butter sauce, I melt half a stick of butter and add salt, pepper, and a teaspoon of lemon juice.

ZUCCHINI

In Egypt, where I spent some of the time when I was a child, we not only ate the zucchini but also the zucchini flower; and the flower was my favorite part. We used to cook the flowers in boiling water, drain them, and serve them in a salad. Once, on Long Island, when I was spending the summer in East Hampton, I saw a farm with a sign saying that we could pick any vegetable that we wanted for a price. I wanted to pick zucchini; and as I went through rows and rows of zucchini plants, lo and behold, I saw a lot of zucchini flowers. And I said, oh, I haven't eaten zucchini flowers for such a long time, and I started to pick them. Well, if I may tell you the truth, I nearly ended up in jail. For in

I started to pick them.

this country, the zucchini flowers are not sold; and behind every zucchini flower there was a zucchini waiting to grow. I was ruining the crop.

When you buy zucchini, never choose those that are very big. The squash should be about four to five inches long and no more than an inch in diameter; if they are bigger, the inside, which has seeds, is overpowering and the vegetable can never really be served nice and crisp.

ZUCCHINI AU GRATIN

WHAT DO YOU NEED?

**6 zucchini
Salt and pepper
1 tablespoon olive oil
1 teaspoon chopped fresh oregano or fresh basil
1 tablespoon bread crumbs
2 tablespoons grated Swiss cheese
Small pats butter**

Wash the zucchini and peel with a potato peeler. In a large saucepan, cook the zucchini in boiling salted water for 7–8 minutes, until they are tender but still very crisp. Drain the zucchini, and cool them. Pat them dry, for the zucchini have a lot of water to begin with. Put them very close together in a buttered shallow baking dish. Add a little bit of salt and pepper. Sprinkle the olive oil over the squash, add the oregano or the basil, and sprinkle with the bread crumbs. On top of the bread crumbs, add the grated cheese and a couple of pieces of butter. Bake in the oven at 350°, until the cheese gets melted and light brown. Serve piping hot.

ENDIVE

Endive is a small, sleek leafy vegetable, and it is a specialty of Belgium. Belgian endives are very thick and very white. Endives are often served in salads; but, among vegetables, braised endive is food for the gods.

BRAISED ENDIVE

WHAT DO YOU NEED?

½ stick butter (4 tablespoons)
6 endives
2 teaspoons sugar
Juice of ½ lemon
Salt and pepper

In a heavy saucepan, melt the butter. When the butter starts to bubble, add the endives and brown them on all sides, turning them carefully with two forks, so they do not fall apart. Sprinkle the endive with the sugar, add the lemon juice, salt, and pepper; cover and simmer until tender. The endives are ready when easily pierced with a fork. Serve this vegetable in a hot dish, and you will get only compliments.

ENDIVE WITH PARSNIPS

In France, endives are also often cooked with parsnips. In this country, parsnips are used today only in soup; but, 400 years ago in Europe, parsnips had the role the potato fills now. A parsnip is a long yellow root vegetable that looks like an overgrown carrot. You have to peel it. When you cook endive, you can add two or three parsnips—washed, peeled, and sliced lengthwise into two or three pieces—and cook the parsnips exactly as you do the endives. The parsnips might take a little bit longer to cook; so, if you are in a hurry, you could parboil the parsnips. Cook the pared, sliced parsnips in boiling water for 8–10 minutes until they are barely done. Then drain them and sauté them with your endive. When you serve this pair, sprinkle them with chopped parsley.

MUSHROOMS

In France, there are a hundred different kinds of mushrooms; and we cook them in many different ways and serve them with different dishes. Here in the United States, the most common mushroom is what we call in France *champignon de Paris*. I love mushrooms. They are my passion. Once, when I spent the summer in Guatemala City, on the last day I went to the central market; and there I saw a stand with three or four different kinds of mushrooms. I lost my head. I bought a couple of pounds of each different kind. As we landed in New York, and I was going through customs, I was stopped and made to throw away all my mushrooms—you are not allowed to bring such things into the country that way. I felt terrible. All during the flight, I had been dreaming of different ways of preparing those lovely mushrooms.

If you know something about mushrooms, you may be able to grow other varieties; but in the supermarket you will find only those whitish, light-brown mushrooms. When you buy mushrooms, the caps and the stems should be smooth and unblem-

*I was dreaming of different
ways of preparing mushrooms.*

ished, fresh-looking, and smelling good. A mushroom that has dark brown spots is too old and not good at all.

SAUTÉED MUSHROOMS WITH CREAM

WHAT DO YOU NEED?

½ pound fresh whole mushrooms, medium-sized
1 tablespoon vinegar
2 tablespoons butter
1 teaspoon oil
2 tablespoons chopped shallots
½ cup heavy cream, whipped
A pinch ground pepper
Salt to taste
Chopped fresh parsley

Wash your mushrooms carefully. Soak them in water with a tablespoon of vinegar. Mushrooms, like asparagus, and many other vegetables, are often full of sand. Don't peel the mushrooms; just cut the tough bottoms of the stems off. In a heavy skillet, melt the butter and the oil. When the oil and the butter are

VEGETABLES

123

very hot, put your mushrooms in and sauté them for 4–5 minutes. Add the shallots, and cook for another 2 minutes.

Whip the heavy cream. Turn off the heat, stir the cream into the mushrooms. Correct the seasoning, adding some freshly ground pepper, salt, and some fresh chopped parsley. Serve immediately. Mushrooms are a good accompaniment to almost any dish. They are good with chicken, with beef, surrounding asparagus or a cauliflower.

POTATOES

There are hundreds of different recipes for potatoes. You can bake potatoes, purée potatoes, fry potatoes, hash-brown potatoes. The following are a couple of recipes that I favor for potatoes.

NEW POTATOES

Spring and summer potatoes are very small, and they are delicious just boiled. When you buy new potatoes, their skin is so thin that by washing them with a brush under running water, it can easily be rubbed off. You do not peel new potatoes.

WHAT DO YOU NEED?

18–24 tiny new potatoes
Salt
2 tablespoons butter
1 tablespoon chopped parsley

In a saucepan, cover your potatoes with boiling water. Add salt. Boil the potatoes until they are done; you know that they are done when they can be pierced easily with a fork. Don't overcook potatoes; they will fall apart. Drain the potatoes. In the saucepan, melt the butter. When the butter is piping hot, return your potatoes to the saucepan, sprinkle with parsley, and sauté the potatoes at a high heat for 2 or 3 minutes. Serve immediately.

FRENCH FRIED POTATOES

To make real French fried potatoes, you need a deep-fat fryer—a heavy saucepan with a basket, which we call in French *une friteuse.* You count one potato per person. They have to be big potatoes. You can cook about three at a time. Wash the potatoes first; peel them with a potato peeler and put them in cold water. If you don't do that, if you don't cover them with cold water as you peel them, your potatoes will turn brown. Slice your potatoes ¼" thick one way first. Then cut each slice in ½" strips, putting them in cold water again until they are all cut. Drain the potatoes and put them in a paper towel and pat them dry. Heat oil in the heavy saucepan. Put your potatoes in the basket (see illustration). When the oil is very hot (370° on a frying thermometer), slowly lower your basket into the oil. Move quickly away; the oil will splatter, and you might get burned. Let the potatoes cook like this for 5–8 minutes, until they are slightly brown. Lift the basket again. Reduce the heat under the oil, and let the potatoes rest in the basket for 5–10 minutes. Then, when you are ready to serve the dinner, heat the oil to 370° again, and drop your basket of potatoes back into the oil. The potatoes will very quickly turn golden brown. Drain them on a paper towel, sprinkle them with salt, and serve immediately. These are real French fries.

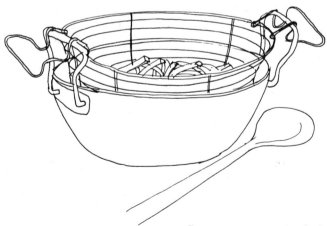

Put your potatoes in the basket.

MASHED POTATOES

Mashed potatoes are very easy to make. But to make a *tasty* mashed potato needs more care. One of the things I usually do when I cook potatoes for mashing is to boil the potatoes in bouillon, which means that to each cup and a half of water I add one bouillon cube.

WHAT DO YOU NEED?

6 potatoes
Beef bouillon (made with cubes)
3 tablespoons butter
Salt and pepper
1 egg
Parsley sprigs

Peel your potatoes. Wash them. Quarter them. In a heavy saucepan, cover your potatoes with bouillon. Boil the potatoes until they fall apart when pricked with a fork. Pour off the bouillon and mash the potatoes with either a potato masher or a fork. Add a tablespoon or two of the bouillon, until you have the right consistency—not too thick, and not too liquid. Pour the potatoes back into the saucepan. Add the butter. Put on a very low flame. Keep on stirring. Break an egg into the mashed potatoes, and stir very quickly. Add freshly ground pepper. Taste to see that the seasoning is correct, and serve, in a pretty dish, with a piece of parsley in the center.

GRATIN DAUPHINOIS

In France, again, everybody has a recipe for potatoes *au gratin*. *Gratin Dauphinois* is made of sliced potatoes, with grated cheese and milk, and usually a pinch of garlic. It is baked in the oven.

WHAT DO YOU NEED?

2 pounds boiling potatoes
½ clove garlic
4 tablespoons butter
Salt and pepper to taste
1 cup grated Swiss cheese
1 cup boiling milk

Peel the potatoes and slice them about ⅛″ thick. Leave them, until you are ready to use them, in a pan of cold water, so that they won't get brown. Preheat the oven to 400°. Rub a baking dish with garlic. The garlic is just really to give a hint of taste. I sometimes take a couple of potatoes and rub them with garlic when I make my layers. Spread at least one tablespoon of butter all over the dish, as if you were preparing a pie. Drain the potatoes, and dry them well with paper towels. Take half the potatoes and spread them in a shallow baking dish. Add salt, pepper, half the cheese, and half the butter in small pieces. Put the remaining potatoes on top of the first layer. Season again with salt and pepper, and spread the rest of the cheese and the butter over it. Now you might take a couple of the potato slices on top and rub some garlic on them. Pour the cup of boiling milk into the potatoes. Bake for at least 30 minutes at 400°, until the potatoes are tender, they have absorbed the milk, and the top slices are nicely brown. Sometimes, I make one layer of potato, one layer of sliced onion, then the grated cheese, and I repeat a layer of potato, etc., with the milk. It's a different type of dish but just as good.

RICE

In certain countries all over the world, rice is the equivalent of the potato in the United States. It is the staple food. In Egypt we ate a lot of rice, and I learned very young how to cook rice. When rice is cooked, it should never be like a mush. The grains should be separate, tender, and fluffy. The rice I usually use is either converted rice or long-grain Carolina rice.

1 tablespoon oil
1½ cups rice
4 cups boiling water
1 teaspoon salt

In a heavy skillet, heat the oil. Pour your rice into the hot oil, and with a wooden spoon stir continuously until the rice starts to bubble and puff up. Then add the boiling water. Add the salt, and with a wooden spoon mix well. Cover and reduce the heat, and simmer for 25–30 minutes. If after 25 minutes you taste the rice and it is still a little bit hard, add ¼ cup water. Cover and continue to cook for another 10 minutes. Your rice should be fluffy, crisp, and delightful. It is marvelous to serve with any meat that has a sauce or with a steak.

5 SALADS

Anyone who could make such a good tomato salad was worth bringing back to the United States.

Salads are very important. A good salad makes a good cook. When we were young, each one of us had a responsibility in the kitchen. Mine was salads, and my mother always said that a salad prepared you for the dessert. It had to be crisp, tangy, and pleasant to eat. After a good meal, when you felt full, it would refresh you and prepare you for the dessert. My husband jokingly says that he married me because of my salads, especially my tomato salad. He felt that anyone who could make such a good tomato salad was worth bringing back to the United States.

SALADS

There are many different kinds of salads. There are green salads, white salads (such as endive), and vegetable salads that can be served as a whole lunch or dinner, with some cold meat, on a hot summer day. As I mentioned earlier, the French never throw away any cooked vegetable; all vegetables that are cooked and remain from the previous dinner are served the next day with vinaigrette. Any dried beans can be made into a salad. There are also many different dressings that you can use—a vinegar dressing, a lemon one, dressing made with mustard, with cheese. One thing I do not like is bottled salad dressing. It is so easy and so quick to make a dressing that there is no reason to buy a prepared one.

When you buy salad greens, you must be careful that the leaves are not overgrown or the outer leaves wilted. Leaves of whatever salad greens you buy should be crisp, fresh, and bright in color.

ICEBERG LETTUCE

Iceberg lettuce is the most common salad green in the United States. When you buy it, squeeze the head. It should be very firm and very tightly packed. The outer leaves should be dark green (though those leaves are not to be used in the salad). Cut off the stem and remove the first few outer leaves. The nicest way to serve an iceberg lettuce is to cut the head in eight parts and leave them whole, not shredded. Put the wedges in individual bowls, two pieces per person; pour over a vinaigrette sauce and sprinkle with chopped fresh parsley.

VINAIGRETTE

You made this sauce for your appetizers (see page 74).

1 teaspoon salt
1 teaspoon pepper
3 tablespoons wine vinegar
¾ cup oil (olive oil, vegetable oil, or peanut oil)

In a bowl put the salt, the pepper, and the vinegar, and mix well so that the salt will really melt in the vinegar. Add the oil. Mix well. This is the basic vinaigrette.

What you do next is take a leaf of the salad and with the leaf stir the sauce and then eat the leaf to taste the sauce. See if there is enough salt and pepper, or vinegar, or oil. If not, add more. Pour the vinaigrette over the iceberg lettuce at the last moment. Sauces for salads should always be poured at the last moment when you are ready to serve. Then sprinkle on top of the iceberg lettuce some chopped parsley.

BOSTON LETTUCE

This is my favorite salad, and it is also the favorite of Cécile—my youngest daughter. She thinks it melts in your mouth. When you buy Boston lettuce, the leaves should not be packed tightly together as in the iceberg lettuce. The head should be like an open rose. The outer leaves should not be too overgrown; that would mean that the Boston lettuce is old. The inner part of the lettuce, the heart, should be crisp, yellow, and very tender.

Cut off the stem of the Boston lettuce. Separate all the leaves. Wash well. Let it drain in a colander; or, if you have one of those mesh baskets, put the leaves in the basket and let it drain so that there is no water left in the salad. In France we put the lettuce in the mesh basket (see next page), and then one of us was always sent outside to shake it. We would shake it and shake it and shake it. Today they have the same basket with a twirl in the center like a top, which you can whirl in the sink.

*One of us was always
sent outside to shake it.*

The best sauce for a Boston lettuce is a vinaigrette. Follow the recipe on page 131, but to the Boston lettuce dressing add a teaspoon of fresh chopped tarragon or basil or chives. Boston lettuce requires nothing more. It is delicate, and therefore the sauce has to be very delicate.

Put the washed Boston lettuce in a salad bowl, and prepare the sauce in a small bowl. If the salad leaves are too big, tear them with your hands—don't cut them with a knife. The French say that you should be able to pick up each piece of salad and eat it without cutting it, so make the pieces bite-sized. Leave the little heart made up of the last few leaves as is. Don't separate them. Maybe you'll be the lucky one, and you will get the heart when you help yourself to the salad.

ROMAINE

Romaine is a long-leafed salad that looks like an overgrown cucumber; the outer leaves are often quite tough and not very tasty. Break them off and throw them away.

Cut off the stem and peel its outside; cut the stem in small pieces and put them in your bowl. They are quite good in a salad. Wash the salad very carefully and tear each outer leaf in three or four pieces. As you get to the heart, you will only need to tear each leaf in half. With romaine, I always add some sliced cucumber and celery. (I never mix any tomatoes with greens in salads. Tomatoes should be served in salads by themselves or with other vegetables.)

WHAT DO YOU NEED?

1 crouton with garlic
1 cup vinaigrette (see page 131)
1 romaine lettuce
2 sticks celery, peeled and sliced thin
1 cucumber, peeled and sliced

What is a crouton with garlic? If you have a loaf of French or Italian bread, take the end part the Americans call the "heel" of the loaf. It is called *le crouton* in French. Peel a garlic clove, and rub the crouton with garlic. Make your vinaigrette sauce, and put the garlicked crouton in it to marinate. At the last minute—just before you pour the vinaigrette over the romaine lettuce, cucumber, and celery—remove the crouton. You may, if you like more garlic, chop the clove of garlic and add it to the vinaigrette instead. I like romaine with vinaigrette and tarragon, too.

TOMATO SALAD

A tomato salad is a glorious thing, especially in the summer, when the tomatoes are plump, red, and juicy. Their taste is fantastic. At the beginning of the meal or at the end, nothing is more refreshing than a delightful tomato salad.

When you buy tomatoes, they have to be bright red, firm and not mushy, with no black spots, but ripe. Tomatoes that are hard and a pale pink-red usually have been picked when they were green and do not have good flavor. The best way to make a tomato salad is to peel the tomatoes. How do you peel tomatoes? In the summer, when the tomatoes are very ripe, they are easy to peel. Boil some water and with a fork dip each tomato in the boiling water for a few seconds. The skin will slide very easily as you peel it by pulling off with a knife.

Another way to peel a tomato is to spear the tomato with a fork; holding the fork, put the tomato over the flame of a gas burner on your stove and turn it to heat all sides. Be careful—you can be burned if the fork gets too hot. What happens is that the skin quickly burns, pops, and splits, and slides off easily when you pull it with a knife. When you have peeled the tomatoes, put them in the refrigerator to cool, before you slice them to make the salad.

In the winter, the tomatoes are not as ripe; therefore it is more difficult to peel them, and you could just slice them very thin and the salad will be almost as good. A tomato salad can be prepared some time before dinner, because tomatoes that are marinated in the sauce are even better.

WHAT DO YOU NEED?

1 cup vinaigrette (see page 131)
1 onion, a sweet one preferably, peeled and sliced thin
1 clove garlic, crushed
6 tomatoes, peeled or unpeeled, and sliced
1 teaspoon dried tarragon
1 tablespoon chopped fresh tarragon, basil, or parsley

Prepare vinaigrette and add dried tarragon. Slice the onion and crush the garlic. Mix well with the sauce in your salad bowl. Let stand for 10 minutes so that the onion and garlic will really be marinated in the vinegar. Peel and slice the tomatoes. Once the tomatoes are peeled, try to slice them holding them over the bowl in which you are going to serve the salad, so that all the juice of the tomatoes drips down and will be mixed up in the vinaigrette. Mix the salad well and sprinkle some fresh chopped tarragon or some fresh chopped basil or parsley on the salad. You will only get compliments. You might even find a nice boy or girl friend.

The sauce of the tomato salad is so good that, after we have cleared the table and there is some sauce of the tomato salad left, I often catch one of my children eating the sauce in the kitchen.

EnDIVE

You have learned in the previous chapter how to cook endive as a vegetable. But endives are also delicious in a salad. When you buy endives, they have to be firm and the leaves very tight. Slice the stem off, and wash the endive; let drain in a colander. There are different ways of serving endive salads. You can serve endive with watercress or serve it with beets and hard-boiled eggs. With endive salads, I do not serve a vinaigrette. I make a lemon sauce.

LEMON SAUCE

WHAT DO YOU NEED?

1 teaspoon each: salt and pepper
Juice of 1 lemon
¾ cup oil (olive oil, vegetable oil, or peanut oil)
1 clove of garlic, crushed

As for the vinaigrette, start with the salt and pepper. Add the lemon and garlic. Mix well. Then add the oil. How do you serve the endive? If you are going to serve the salad by itself, cut the endive lengthwise, and then cut the halves into about 1″ pieces. Put the slices into the salad bowl. Pour over the lemon sauce, and mix well. As for Boston lettuce or any other lettuce, pour the sauce at the last moment. To make the salad even more interesting, I add a bunch of watercress.

WATERCRESS AND ENDIVE SALAD

Watercress comes in a bunch. The leaves are dark green and small. If they are very big, the watercress is often too strong in taste. Try to choose watercress with smaller leaves that are dark green. Cut off the lower stems and wash the watercress very well. Let it drain in the colander. At the last moment, put the endive and the watercress in the salad bowl; pour in the lemon sauce, mix well, and serve immediately.

ENDIVE WITH BEETS AND HARD-BOILED EGGS

WHAT DO YOU NEED?

**1-pound can whole beets
6 endives
1 cup vinaigrette (see page 131)
1 clove garlic, crushed
3 hard-boiled eggs
2 tablespoons chopped fresh parsley**

Drain the beets. Slice them very thin. Wash the endive and, this time, don't cut it lengthwise but separate each leaf and leave it whole. Mix the endive leaves and the sliced beets together. Pour over the vinaigrette sauce to which you have added the crushed garlic. Mix well. Slice the hard-boiled eggs and make a design with the egg slices on top of the salad. Sprinkle some fresh parsley leaves and serve. (Don't mix in the hard-boiled eggs; they will crumble and become mushy.) This is a very beautiful-looking salad: the white of the endive, the red of the beets, the yellow and the white of the hard-boiled eggs, the bright-green parsley.

CHICORY

Chicory is a lettuce whose leaves are all curly. The outer leaves are dark green; and, as you get to the center, they become pale yellow. Chicory is often overgrown; so you must be very careful when you buy a chicory that the leaves are small, not too long, and that the center of the chicory is really yellow. This is a slightly bitter salad green; and, therefore, it needs a different dressing. I serve it with a vinaigrette made with croutons and bacon.

WHAT DO YOU NEED?

3 slices of white bread
3 slices of bacon
½ teaspoon salt
½ teaspoon pepper
3 tablespoons vinegar
¼ cup bacon fat instead of oil
1 head chicory
Garlic

Make the croutons by cutting each slice of bread into five long strips and each strip in little cubes. Put the croutons in the oven at 350° for about 6–8 minutes until they are brown but not burned. They will be dry and crisp.

In a frying pan, cook the bacon until it is very crisp. Drain it on a paper towel; and when it is cool to the touch, crumble it. Save the bacon fat to make the vinaigrette. Start with the salt and pepper—not too much this time. Add the vinegar and three or four tablespoons of the bacon fat. Mix. Taste the sauce; it should not be too greasy. Correct the seasoning.

Break off the outer leaves of the chicory and throw them away. Wash the chicory and break the remaining leaves in small pieces. Put the chicory in a bowl and add the croutons, some rubbed with garlic. Mix well. Pour the sauce in the salad, mix it well. On top of the salad, just before you serve it, put in the center a little pile of crumbled bacon. This is a salad that is made in Normandy with *pissenlit,* dandelion greens.

ESCAROLE

Escarole, like chicory, is a slightly bitter salad. It is very tasty, but needs a stronger dressing. Again, when you buy an escarole, the leaves have to be very crisp. The inner leaves are white and yellow, and they get greener and greener as you get to the outside of the salad. Pull off the outer leaves (you can cook them and then serve them cold as a vegetable salad). The larger escarole leaves are long, so break them off in three or four pieces, making all the pieces the same size as you work toward the small ones in the center. Wash and drain the escarole and serve it with a mustard vinaigrette, with a clove of garlic.

MUSTARD VINAIGRETTE

This is a stronger salad dressing that is very good on escarole.

WHAT DO YOU NEED?

1 tablespoon Dijon mustard
¾ cup oil (olive oil, vegetable oil, or peanut oil)
¼ cup vinegar
Salt and pepper
1 clove garlic, chopped very fine (optional)

This time start with the mustard. Put the mustard in the bowl and, as if you were making a mayonnaise, with a wooden spoon beat in the oil until the mustard doubles in volume. Then add the vinegar. Add the vinegar slowly and taste it sometimes, so that your salad dressing is not too strong. Add salt and pepper to taste. Then add to the mustard dressing the garlic. (The garlic is optional. If you are not very fond of garlic, you don't have to use it. I like garlic, and as a young girl after school I used to eat garlic and bread. Everybody used to run away from me. My children like garlic too; but it has a strong taste, and you need a box of mints after dinner.)

Put your salad in a bowl and at the last minute pour over the dressing. Mix well and serve immediately.

SALAD DRESSINGS

There are other dressings that you can make for different salads. You can add cheeses, curry, anchovies, capers, etc. Here are a couple of dressings which are good with any salad except Boston lettuce, which is very delicate and needs the very delicate dressing.

ROQUEFORT FRENCH DRESSING

WHAT DO YOU NEED?

¼ teaspoon salt
Black pepper
¼ cup vinegar
½ cup oil
2 tablespoons heavy cream
¼ cup crumbled Roquefort cheese
Lemon juice

Start with the salt and pepper, add the vinegar and the oil. Mix well. Then add the heavy cream and the Roquefort cheese. You have to crumble the Roquefort cheese into little tiny pieces. At the last moment add 3–4 drops of lemon juice. You will see how marvelous this dressing is.

It is important to add your Roquefort dressing to the salad greens at the last minute so they won't become soggy.

HERB FRENCH DRESSING

You can make an herb dressing following the vinaigrette recipe on page 131. To the basic sauce, you will add a tablespoon each of chopped fresh parsley, tarragon, chervil, and chives. The dressing should be really very fragrant with herbs. It is quite nice on a Boston lettuce.

VINAIGRETTE WITH THE JUICE OF A BEEFSTEAK

This is a very satisfactory dressing that I serve on watercress when I cook a steak or a roast beef. You make a vinaigrette, following the recipe on page 131. Add a crushed garlic clove. And, at the last minute, add two or three tablespoons of the drippings from the roast beef or the juice from the pan in which you have cooked the steak. Pour the sauce over the watercress salad. It is an especially good salad to serve if you are serving no vegetables with the steak.

VEGETABLES AS SALADS

As we said in the introduction to this chapter, almost any vegetable, dry or fresh and cooked or raw, is delicious in a salad. Vegetable salads are very good in the summer when it is hot and you don't feel like cooking. Vegetable salads are something that the French always serve as an appetizer with some salami or some prosciutto. They serve all different kinds of vegetables in the vinaigrette: some need onions, some need garlic, some are good with a lemon dressing. The vegetables should always be served very cold; so cook your vegetables the day before, and refrigerate them before you make them into a salad. Also, the vegetables always have to be well drained; there should be no water. The vegetables should be undercooked rather than overcooked.

LEEKS

Leeks are not a very popular vegetable in the United States. They are rather expensive, but sometimes in the summer they are available. In France, leeks are called "the asparagus of the poor"; and leeks with vinaigrette are fantastic.

A leek looks like an overgrown spring onion—a big scallion. The base is white, and as you get to the top it gets greener. Leeks are often full of sand, and they have to be washed very well. First cut off the root ends and remove the outside layer. Then cut leeks lengthwise in many, many slices; and wash them well under running water. Put the washed slices in a saucepan and cover with salted water. Cook until tender. With a slotted spoon remove the leeks and drain them well. Serve with a vinaigrette sauce (page 131) and sprinkle with chopped parsley.

STRING BEANS, BROCCOLI

Those two vegetables, if not overcooked, are delicious in salads. The dressing you put on either the string beans or broccoli is a vinaigrette (page 131) with crushed garlic or a small onion, chopped. What I also like to add to my string bean salad or broccoli salad are some bean sprouts; you can find them almost anywhere today. On top of the cold cooked string beans or broccoli I sprinkle half a cup of washed raw bean sprouts. Don't mix them up with the broccoli or the string beans, because they should be crisp; and they will wilt if you mix them up before you serve them.

LENTILS

Cooked lentils or dried lima beans are very good cold in a salad. They are a fine winter salad, when there are not too many vegetables in season.

3 cups water
1 cup dried lentils
2 teaspoons salt
2 cups sliced cooked smoked sausage
1 clove garlic, chopped
1 cup lemon dressing with garlic (see page 135)
½ cup minced scallions
Chopped parsley

In a large saucepan, cover the lentils with water and add salt. Bring the water to a boil at very high heat. Reduce the heat and simmer the lentils for about 30 minutes. Taste them at 20 minutes. The lentils should be *just* cooked, when you make a salad. Drain the lentils well and refrigerate. In a bowl, combine the sliced sausage and the chopped garlic. Add a cup of lemon dressing; mix well, and pour over the lentils. Add the chopped scallions and mix well again. Sprinkle with minced parsley and serve.

LIMA BEANS OR CHICK PEAS

The same recipe is very good made with dried lima beans or canned lima beans. The lima beans, if they are dried, will need to cook a little bit longer than the lentils. If the beans are in a can, drain them well and then wash them under running water, so that none of the water in which the canned lima beans came remains. Drain well. The sausage is optional. Mix the lima beans with the dressing and the minced scallions and the chopped garlic. Sprinkle with minced parsley and serve.

Another good dried vegetable for salad are chick peas. They come in a can. Drain the peas well and serve them with a lemon sauce (page 135), parsley, and crushed garlic. They are very good with cold meat any time for lunch or dinner.

CAULIFLOWER WITH
VINAIGRETTE AND CAPERS

Cauliflower also is a delicious salad.

WHAT DO YOU NEED?

1 medium head cauliflower, trimmed of leaves and stem
1 teaspoon salt
Vinaigrette (page 131)
10–12 capers
Chopped parsley

In a saucepan, put the whole cauliflower, head down. Cover it with water and add a teaspoon of salt. Put the burner at high heat; and, when the water boils, lower the heat and simmer for about 15–20 minutes. You will know the cauliflower is done when you pierce it with a fork and the fork goes in easily. Drain the cauliflower. Then put it in a bowl, stem down but whole as is, and surround it maybe with a few Boston lettuce leaves. Make a vinaigrette sauce to which you add a dozen capers. Pour the vinaigrette on the cauliflower, sprinkle some chopped parsley, and serve at room temperature.

GREEK SALADS

JULIETTE'S CUCUMBER SALAD
WITH YOGURT

My daughter Juliette went to Crete one summer and came back and endlessly talked about this marvelous cucumber salad with dry yogurt. Well, it is hard to find dry yogurt in the United States (but we finally did); it's slightly more tasty and spicy than regular yogurt. We experimented and found out that we could make a delicious cucumber salad with ordinary yogurt.

3 cucumbers, peeled and diced
2 ½-pint containers plain yogurt
3 cloves garlic peeled and crushed
Juice of 1 lemon
Salt and pepper to taste
1 pinch ground cumin
Dried thyme or fresh mint

Peel and dice the cucumbers. Sprinkle some salt on the cubes and let them stand. Meanwhile, in a bowl, beat with a fork the two containers of yogurt. Add the fresh garlic, the lemon juice, salt and pepper, a pinch of cumin, and ¼ teaspoon dried thyme. Or replace the thyme with fresh mint. Drain the cucumbers, add them to the yogurt mixture, refrigerate.

Serve with *pita* bread, warmed in the oven. We ate this combination nearly every day this summer, as Juliette became an expert in making Greek salads.

JULIETTE'S GREEK SALAD

On Crete, Juliette stayed in a house overlooking the sea; and next door was a Greek family where the mother-in-law screamed rather a lot. To have some silence, Juliette's hosts invited the mother-in-law to their house and Juliette praised her salad and asked her how she made it. So the neighbor came and made the salad and they became friends and they had peace and quiet for the next three weeks. Coming back to the United States, Juliette reproduced that marvelous salad for us.

WHAT DO YOU NEED?

½ Boston lettuce
3 tomatoes
1 cucumber
1 green pepper

5–6 black olives
1 clove garlic, crushed
½ cup lemon dressing (see page 135)
1 piece (about 4 ounces) Greek feta cheese, crumbled

Wash the lettuce and break it in small pieces. Drain. Put the lettuce in a bowl; add to it the tomatoes, peeled and quartered; the cucumber, peeled and sliced; the pepper, seeded and sliced thin; the black olives; and the garlic, crushed. Pour the lemon dressing over the salad. Toss well, and add, as you are about to serve, the crumbled feta cheese on top.

SALADE NIÇOISE

A *salade niçoise* is a meal in itself. It is often served at lunch; or for dinner, if you have a nice soup, you could serve a *salade niçoise* with maybe a couple of slices of ham or cold roast beef.

WHAT DO YOU NEED?

1 Boston lettuce
1 3-ounce can tuna fish
4 hard-boiled eggs
2 tomatoes
12 small new potatoes
½ pound green beans
8 anchovy filets, each rolled with a caper in the center
Capers
Greek black cured olives
Green olives
Mustard dressing, about 1½ cups (see page 138)

Wash the Boston lettuce and drain well. In a big glass bowl, spread the lettuce leaves. Then drain the tuna fish and separate it into small pieces; put them on top of the Boston lettuce. Arrange tomato slices on top of the tuna fish. Peel the hard-boiled eggs, cut them in half, and put them on top of the tomatoes. Boil 12 small new potatoes in salted water until tender, drain, peel them and halve them, and arrange them over the hard-boiled eggs. Boil the string beans, cut in ½ inch pieces, in salted water until just tender; drain. Add the cooked string beans to the salad while they are still warm; don't cool them. Add the anchovy filets; and sprinkle on top of the whole salad some capers, the black olives, and the green olives. Pour the mustard dressing on top of everything. The salad should not be mixed; it should look like layers of color. Sometimes I also add some cooked red peppers that are marinated; they come in a can, and I cut them twice and sprinkle a couple of them around. You need a lot of color. You can add some sliced radishes, too. It's a very hearty salad.

POTATO SALAD

Here is a salad that can be made with cold boiled potatoes, when you have some new potatoes that remain from the previous dinner; but I like to make my potato salad with potatoes that I boil especially for that purpose. When you make a potato salad while the potatoes are still warm, and you pour the dressing on the warm potatoes, the potatoes absorb the dressing and taste much better and not at all oily.

WHAT DO YOU NEED?

8 medium-sized potatoes, peeled
1 teaspoon salt
1 cup vinaigrette with mustard (see page 138)
5 shallots, peeled and chopped
¼ cup chopped fresh parsley

In a heavy saucepan, cover the peeled potatoes with water and add salt. Bring to a boil, reduce the heat, and let simmer for 15–25 minutes, until the potatoes are tender (you know it by piercing them with a fork). Don't let the potatoes fall apart; they will, if they are overcooked. Meanwhile, in a bowl, make the mustard vinaigrette following the recipe on page 138. I sometimes add a teaspoon of lemon juice. Then peel and chop the shallots. Add them to the dressing. Then chop the parsley and add it to the dressing. Drain the potatoes and let them cool just until you can handle them. Slice the potatoes about ¼″ thick and mix them in the dressing delicately, so that they will not fall apart. Sometimes to decorate, once the potatoes are dressed, I add a couple of slices of hard-boiled eggs sprinkled with parsley. Refrigerate and, when cooled, serve.

6 POULTRY, MEATS, AND FISH

This is the last chapter of our book. When you have gone through this chapter, you will be *un grand chef* and able to follow any recipe you wish. It's fun to cook, and it is even more fun to do main courses—for they are really the most important part of a meal. What one can do with chicken or turkey is endless; what one can do with hamburger, beef chuck, or any kind of beef is also endless. The principle in this chapter is to learn how to cook these meats and then—using your knowledge, or what you might have read somewhere else, to change a recipe here and there—to experiment. Remember that what counts is what you taste and that your ideas are certainly great; if you want to add something, to use a meat in a different way, try it. You might create a brand-new recipe.

POULTRY

CHICKEN

Chicken in the United States is plentiful, and it is here still quite reasonable to buy. In France, chickens are very expensive, and we don't serve chicken very often. Usually chicken is reserved for Sunday lunch, which is an important meal; because either you invite your friends, or you gather your family around you. But in this country, we can perform miracles with chicken.

How to buy a chicken: There are many different sorts of chickens. Broilers, which are small and young, weigh from ¾ of a pound to 2½ pounds and are often split in two down the back. Fryers, a little larger, are up to 3½ pounds; these are usually cut in 4 to 8 pieces. Another chicken is the roaster. It's usually a heavier chicken; its breast is bigger, and it often weighs between 2½ and 5 pounds; it is sold whole.

In supermarkets, chickens are sold ready to use. They are plucked and the innards removed; and the giblets, which are the neck, stomach, heart, and liver, are in a separate little bag. When I was a little girl, chickens were sold alive, feathers and all. My mother always told the poultry man, "I hope it has an egg inside; it's for Colette." I used to love to find the egg, usually with no shell. My mother would poach it for me.

Another chicken is a capon, which is a male bird that has been castrated. It is certainly, if one is roasting a chicken, the best. It is also the most expensive, because it is much bigger—it often weighs from 4 to 8 pounds. And then you have, if you can find it, a large hen or fowl. It is an older chicken; it is a tough bird, and you cannot use it to roast or to broil. A fowl is used for stewing, braising, or to make a soup. A stewing chicken weighs from 2½ to 5 pounds. Its color is different also: Instead of being a sort of light, bright yellow, the skin is whiter; and the bird definitely has less tender meat. In general, choose a chicken that has short legs and a plump body, and make sure that its skin is unbruised. A good layer of fat covering the breast, or the inside of the chicken, is certainly an indication that it is a young chicken, and therefore the meat is going to be tender.

Chickens that are roasted can be stuffed, but remember these principles in stuffing the bird. One, don't stuff the bird until it is

"I hope it has an egg inside."

ready to roast. If you have to prepare the meal in advance, keep the bird and the stuffing separate until you are ready to roast. Two, don't overstuff a chicken; because stuffing expands during the roasting, and it will not be as tasty if the juice of the chicken does not reach the center part of the stuffing.

Basic preparation for cooking a chicken, regardless of the recipe you will select: Rinse the chicken in cold running water. Drain it, and dry it with paper towels. Take a lemon, cut it in two, and rub the chicken in and out with the lemon. This is very good; because most chickens have been kept on ice, or are sold in plastic bags, and it will refresh the chicken and give it a lovely taste if it is rubbed with lemon before you prepare it.

To roast a chicken, you buy either a roasting chicken or a whole broiler; a nice-sized broiler will do as well as a roasting chicken, and it is more reasonable in price.

ROAST CHICKEN

WHAT DO YOU NEED?

1 chicken, 3½ to 4 pounds
4 tablespoons butter
1 teaspoon salt
1 teaspoon pepper
1 teaspoon dried tarragon
2 cups boiling water
1 chicken bouillon cube

Preheat your oven at 350°. Wash and prepare the chicken as above. With your finger, separate the skin from the breast, as if to make a little pocket. Put a tablespoon of butter in each pocket; press it down with your hand to spread it. With the remaining butter, spread one tablespoon inside the chicken; and with your hand rub the skin of the chicken with the rest of the butter. Sprinkle the buttered bird with salt, pepper, and tarragon. Place the chicken in an open shallow pan, on a rack if you have one; put it in the oven, and let it roast for ½ hour. Meanwhile, boil some water; and, in 2 cups of water, dissolve a bouillon cube. After ½ hour, baste the chicken with the bouillon—that means to spoon some of the broth over the top of the bird so that it is moistened all over. Cook the chicken for a total of 1 hour to 1½ hours, basting it every half hour. You will know when the chicken is done: One, it will have a golden color; two, if you move the drumstick (use a potholder or paper towel so you won't burn your fingers) it will move easily. Three, if you take a fork and prick the drumstick, the liquid running out should be clear. If the juice is still bloody, the chicken needs another 10 minutes of cooking. Put the chicken on a platter and surround it with parsley. Add some bouillon or water to the pan juice; correct the seasoning, and let the juices boil for a couple of minutes. Serve in a bowl next to the chicken. It is nice to serve roast chicken with French fried or mashed potatoes and with broccoli.

STUFFED ROAST CHICKEN

WHAT DO YOU NEED?

1 roasting chicken, 3½ to 4 pounds, or a whole broiler
1 lemon
4 tablespoons butter
¾ cup bread crumbs
Liver of the chicken
4 shallots, chopped fine
1 clove garlic, chopped fine
1 teaspoon each, dried parsley, tarragon, thyme, rosemary
3 Italian sausages
3 tablespoons milk
1 egg yolk
Salt and pepper
1 chicken bouillon cube dissolved in 2 cups boiling water

Preheat your oven to 350°. Prepare the chicken as you learned at the beginning of the chapter: wash, rub with lemon and butter (see pages 150–151).

Prepare the stuffing: In a bowl, put the bread crumbs; chop the liver, and add it to the bread crumbs. Chop the shallots and add. Add the garlic and the parsley, tarragon, thyme, and rosemary. Take the meat of the Italian sausages out of the skins. Add the sausage meat to the bread crumbs. Mix well. Use your hands. Add the milk to moisten the stuffing. Then add the egg yolk. Mix well again. Taste the mixture. Add salt and pepper. Mix well again, and taste again. Stuffing should be spicy.

Stuff the open cavity of the chicken, but don't overstuff it. Then close the cavity with skewers and string. Or I find it much quicker and easier to tuck a piece of aluminum foil inside the opening to hold the stuffing in place. Put the chicken on a rack in a shallow pan. Place it in the heated oven, and cook it for 1½ hours or until the chicken is done (test as before, page 151), basting it from time to time with the bouillon.

When you serve the chicken, leave it whole; carve it at the table, giving each person a piece of chicken, some stuffing, and some of the pan juice that you have prepared as on page 151.

Whenever you buy ready-to-cook chickens, in a little bag you will find the giblets—which consist of the gizzard, the neck, the heart, and the liver. The liver can always be used in your stuffing. Now, keep the giblets and neck. You can freeze them. When you have enough giblets, you can make a very good chicken soup following the recipe in Chapter 3 (see page 88). Sometimes you can use that soup instead of the bouillon made from a cube to baste your chicken.

BROILED CHICKEN

To broil a chicken, try to buy young broilers, small ones, for they are much tenderer. You can buy them already cut, or a whole small broiler, 2½ to 3½ pounds, and either have the butcher cut it or cut it yourself into four serving pieces. It is nice to marinate your chicken before you broil it.

Marinade:

WHAT DO YOU NEED?

1 teaspoon salt
1 teaspoon pepper
2 tablespoons vinegar
4 tablespoons oil
1 teaspoon dried tarragon
1 teaspoon chopped fresh parsley (or use dried thyme with the tarragon)

Mix the ingredients well and pour the sauce over the chicken in a bowl; let it stand in the sauce for about 20 minutes to an hour. Preheat the broiler, and place your chicken quarters, skin side down, on the broiler rack (oil the rack first). Place the broiler pan as far away from the heat as possible, because you want the chicken to cook slowly and not to burn. Brush the chicken with the sauce that you have marinated it in from time to time. After 10–15 minutes, turn the chicken the other way and brush with sauce. You will know when the chicken is done by its color and by pricking it with a fork. If the juices, again, come out clear, your chicken is done. If the juice is still bloody, the chicken needs additional cooking.

You can serve this broiled chicken without any sauce, with potatoes, string beans, any vegetable you wish. Or, you can serve it with a barbecue sauce. You can buy the barbecue sauce in bottles, or make it yourself.

BARBECUE SAUCE

WHAT DO YOU NEED?

**1 tablespoon vegetable oil
1 onion, chopped
1 clove of garlic, crushed
1 tablespoon tomato paste
½ cup bouillon
1 tablespoon Worcestershire sauce
½ teaspoon hot pepper sauce, or Tabasco
½ cup fresh lemon juice
½ cup vinegar
Salt and pepper
1 tablespoon brown sugar (optional)**

Heat the oil in a heavy saucepan. Sauté the onion. Add the crushed garlic. Then add the tablespoon of tomato paste; and, after mixing well, add the bouillon. Then add Worcestershire sauce, hot pepper sauce, lemon juice, and vinegar. Let sauce cook for 10–15 minutes. Correct the seasoning. Add some salt and pepper. Sometimes you can add a tablespoon of brown sugar; and what I do, too, which gives a very nice smoky flavor, instead of plain salt, I get hickory-smoked salt, and I use that. When the sauce is cooked, and when the chicken is half-cooked, I brush the sauce on the chicken, while it is broiling, and serve the chicken with some more sauce on the side.

CHICKEN CUTLETS

This is a much more elegant way, maybe more expensive, to serve chicken. This is a recipe that I learned from my grandmother, who had literally a colony of Russian friends. She, in turn, had learned her recipe from those Russian friends. I always used to watch her prepare this dish, for when I was a little girl, I thought she was doing some kind of magic trick; because the chicken, first, did not quite taste like chicken, and second, did not look like chicken.

WHAT DO YOU NEED?

2 large whole chicken breasts, skinned and boned
Salt and pepper
¼ teaspoon ground nutmeg
12 tablespoons butter (1½ sticks)
½ cup flour
2 cups bread crumbs
1 egg
1 tablespoon water
2 tablespoons plus 1 teaspoon oil
¼ cup chopped fresh parsley

You can buy the chicken breasts already boned; you must remove the skin and chop the meat in an electric meat grinder. In a bowl, place the chopped chicken; add salt, pepper, and nutmeg. Melt eight tablespoons of butter; add to the chopped chicken; mix well with a wooden spoon. Put the mixture in the freezer for about 10–15 minutes.

On your table or counter, prepare the following: On one sheet of waxed paper put the flour with some salt and pepper. On another piece of waxed paper, put the bread crumbs. In between these sheets, have a pie plate in which you have beaten the egg with a tablespoon of water, and a teaspoon of oil. Remove the chopped chicken from the freezer, and divide the mixture into eight balls. Shape each ball in the form of a little cutlet. Flatten them a little bit, and start to dip the cutlets, one at a time, first into the flour, then into the egg, and then into the bread crumbs, and put them back on a large plate. Do this for each of the chicken cutlets; then put them back in the freezer for about 10 minutes. In a heavy skillet, melt four tablespoons butter with two tablespoons oil. When this is hot, carefully add the cutlets. Cook until they are golden brown on one side. Then, with a spatula, turn them over and cook them for another 5–6 minutes, until they are also brown on the other side. Arrange on platter; sprinkle with chopped parsley. Serve with lemon-butter sauce.

LEMON-BUTTER SAUCE

WHAT DO YOU NEED?

1 stick butter (8 tablespoons)
¼ cup lemon juice
4 tablespoons chicken bouillon (made with a cube)
Salt and pepper
10 capers cut in small pieces

Cut the butter in eight pieces and refrigerate. In a small heavy saucepan boil the lemon juice until it is reduced to one tablespoon. Remove the pan from the heat and beat in, with a whisk, two pieces of butter. Then replace saucepan on a very low flame and add one piece of butter at a time, beating with a whisk all the time. Stir in the bouillon; add salt and pepper, the chopped capers, and serve immediately.

POULET SAUTÉ

This is a quick way to make a sautéed chicken delicious.

WHAT DO YOU NEED?

5 tablespoons butter
1 chicken, 2½ to 3 pounds, cut in serving pieces
1 tablespoon flour
1½ cups white wine
1 tablespoon dried tarragon
Salt and pepper
Juice of ½ lemon

In a heavy skillet, melt the butter. Sauté the chicken pieces until they are golden colored, for 10–12 minutes. Remove the chicken to a plate; stir the flour into the fat and juice in the skillet; let it brown slightly. Add the white wine and mix well. Cook 2 or 3 minutes. Put the chicken back into the skillet, add the tarragon, salt, and pepper, and cook, covered, for 8–10 minutes (test the chicken by piercing it to make sure it is done). This is a very quick way to cook your chicken. Just before serving, add the lemon juice, and correct the seasoning.

You can elaborate on this recipe. For example, you can replace the white wine with red wine; then add a drained can of little onions and sauté some mushrooms in a tablespoon of butter, and add to your chicken.

Or you can use four or five small potatoes, cut in quarters, added to the sauce.

Or, when you add the flour to your sauce, you can add a tablespoon of tomato paste and some crushed garlic. Then add some sautéed mushrooms and use the white wine to mix the sauce with. If you want to be more elegant, at the last minute you leave out the lemon juice and add half a cup of heavy cream to your sauce. Correct the seasoning.

CHICKEN ROLLED WITH BUTTER AND PEPPER FLAKES

This is another recipe that calls for breast of chicken.

WHAT DO YOU NEED?

3 chicken breasts, boned
3 tablespoons butter
Salt and pepper
2 teaspoons dried green-pepper flakes
Toothpicks
1 egg, beaten with 1 tablespoon water
1 cup flour
½ cup oil
Chopped fresh parsley

Divide each boned chicken breast into two. Wrap each piece in foil or in waxed paper; and, with your heaviest skillet, bang each piece to flatten it. Or, if you have a meat pounder, pound the halves of chicken breasts till they are quite flat. Chill the butter in the freezer until it is very hard. Then take each half of a chicken breast, and into the center put ½ tablespoon of chilled butter, sprinkle it with salt and pepper, and sprinkle it with the green-pepper flakes. Roll the chicken breast tightly around the butter. Close with a toothpick. Roll the chicken in the beaten egg and water, then in the flour. Put the chicken roll on a platter. Repeat this process for each piece of chicken breast. Chill for about 10 minutes in the freezer. Meanwhile, in a heavy skillet, heat the oil; and, when the oil is very hot, quickly fry the chicken rolls until they are golden brown on all sides. Serve on a bed of lettuce, sprinkled with parsley. Serve with sautéed carrots (see page 116).

TURKEY

I still find it quite difficult to eat turkey; for, as a young bride, I had an unforgettable experience. We were living in Italy, and my husband longed for a real Thanksgiving dinner. He explained what a Thanksgiving dinner consisted of, mainly turkey. I promised I would make one.

I went to the central square of this little Italian town, which on Wednesdays held a big market. I found a young boy who had poultry in wooden cages. I asked him if he had a turkey. "Yes," was the answer. After a few moments of bargaining I bought one. Disaster struck! I was handed a beautiful live turkey. What was I to do with it? Kill it? Not I!

After begging the boy for half an hour, I finally persuaded him, for a fee, to kill it—if I helped. Agreed! We went in a dark alley, he with a knife, I, trembling, holding the turkey. While I closed my eyes, slash went the blade. My hands let go, and there was the headless turkey running in circles. Well, it took me a number of years to recover from that experience; but here in the United States you can buy a turkey nicely cleaned and ready to cook.

I found a young boy who had poultry in wooden cages.

One day I sneaked in and looked.

Prepare and stuff a turkey the same way you have done a chicken; but you should, depending on the size of your turkey, increase the amount of stuffing. I also marinate my turkey. This marinade recipe was given to me by Lucy, my housekeeper, who comes from Bogotá in Colombia, where they eat a lot of turkey, because turkey is native to the Americas. She always marinates the turkey for a couple of hours before roasting it, and it is always the best turkey I have ever eaten. For years she would not give me the recipe. Whenever I bought turkey, she would prepare it when she knew I was not in the house. One day I sneaked in and looked, and this is the recipe.

WHAT DO YOU NEED?

1 tablespoon salt
1 tablespoon pepper

2 shallots or 2 small onions, chopped fine
1 clove garlic, chopped fine
1 tablespoon chopped fresh parsley
3 tablespoons vinegar
1 cup dry vermouth or dry white Cinzano
½ teaspoon ground cumin

Mix all the ingredients in a bowl. Wash your turkey (about 10 pounds) as you have done for a chicken. Pat it dry, rub it with a lemon cut in two, inside and out, place it in a roasting pan, and pour this mixture over the turkey. From time to time, baste it again. Let it stand for a couple of hours, turning the turkey or basting the turkey with this juice. When you are ready to roast the turkey, unstuffed, place between the turkey breast and the skin two or three tablespoons of butter.

Preheat your oven at 350°. Put your turkey in the oven, and let it cook for about ¾ of an hour, basting it once or twice with the sauce that it was marinated in. When the breast of the turkey starts to get a golden color, cover it loosely with a piece of aluminum foil, and let the bird cook for another hour. Remove the foil. Check your turkey, by pricking and wiggling the drumstick. It will probably need another half hour of cooking. Now you can remove the foil. If the pan juice starts to dry up, add one or two cups of bouillon and continue to baste your turkey. This turkey is delicious. Eat it cold or hot.

You can stuff the turkey the same way you have stuffed the chicken; depending upon the size of the turkey, double or triple the stuffing recipe.

GOOSE

In France and in England, instead of turkey (the French word for turkey is marvelous; it's called *dindon*), we often eat goose. Geese are harder to find in the United States; they do exist, but they often are frozen. You have to defrost your goose. These geese are sometimes not as tender as European geese, but they can be delicious. One reason I like to cook a goose for Christmas is that the fat that the goose has inside its cavity can be melted and then kept in the refrigerator for a couple of months. It is delicious to use in cooking hash-brown potatoes, or such vegetables as broccoli or brussels sprouts.

How to prepare a goose: If you have bought a frozen goose, you have to let it defrost, in a dish, for at least twenty-four hours. Wash your goose under running cold water. Pat it dry with paper towels. Remove all the loose pieces of fat that you will find inside the goose.

Take ¼ cup of coarse salt, which is often, in the United States, kosher salt; add to the salt six cloves of garlic, chopped. Mix well, and rub your goose with the salt and garlic, inside and out. Let the goose stand for a couple of hours, coated with salt and garlic.

Meanwhile, cut the goose fat in small pieces. Chop a medium-sized onion, skin and all; and, in a heavy skillet, melt the goose fat with the onion, sautéing until the goose fat and the onion are a dark golden brown. When the fat has cooled, strain the liquid into a clean empty coffee can that has a lid, and refrigerate; you can keep the fat for months, using a tablespoon at a time for sautéing, as I said, brussels sprouts or hash-brown potatoes, or any other vegetable you wish. The cracklings, which are strained-out goose fat and onion, sprinkled with salt, are delicious on a piece of bread.

STUFFED ROAST GOOSE

WHAT DO YOU NEED?

1 goose (9 to 10 pounds)
Kosher salt
Garlic, chopped fine

¼ cup chopped fresh parsley
2 tablespoons dried tarragon
4 cups bread crumbs
Goose liver, chopped
3 chicken livers, chopped
1 stick butter (8 tablespoons)
10 shallots, chopped
2 eggs
6 Italian sausages
Salt and pepper to taste
2 tablespoons brandy (optional)
3 cloves garlic, plus finely chopped garlic
2 cups chicken bouillon (made with cubes)
Parsley

Prepare the goose with the coarse salt and the chopped garlic, as described on page 162. Cut off the neck skin; you will use it later. In a bowl, mix the parsley, tarragon, and bread crumbs. Add chopped goose liver and chopped chicken livers. In a heavy skillet, melt the butter. Sauté the chopped shallots. When they are transparent, add them to the bread crumbs. Add two whole eggs. Mix well. Remove the skins of the Italian sausages; cut or crumble the meat in little pieces. Add to the stuffing. Mix well. Taste the stuffing; it might need some salt or pepper. I also add sometimes two tablespoons brandy. Stuff the goose lightly. Close the opening with aluminum foil.

Take cloves of garlic and cut them in three or four pieces lengthwise. Make some slits with a small knife in the breast of the goose and insert the garlic slivers. Prick the entire goose with a fork. A goose is very fat, and you have to allow the fat to melt and run off while the bird is cooking. Preheat your oven at 350°. Place your goose on a rack in a roasting pan. Add a cup of water, and roast for an hour, basting frequently. An hour later, with a bulb baster remove the juice in the pan, which will be mainly goose fat. This goose fat also can be stored in the refrigerator and kept for later use. Add to your pan two cups of bouillon, and cook your goose for another ¾ of an hour, basting it frequently. Serve the goose on a platter, surrounded with parsley. Serve it with sautéed brussels sprouts, or broccoli, and braised endive. This is a very festive dish.

Stuffing the neck: Cut the neck skin away from the goose. Lay it flat, and remove the veins and the fat inside the skin. (See illustration.) Fold the skin in two. Start sewing it, using heavy thread in a darning needle and starting from the narrow end; leave the wider end open to stuff. When you are stuffing your goose, save ¾ cup of stuffing to stuff the neck skin. When it is stuffed, sew the last opening (see illustration). Roast the neck skin alongside the goose; and, when the goose is cooked, remove the neck, let it cool, refrigerate, and serve as an appetizer, sliced very thin, with mustard.

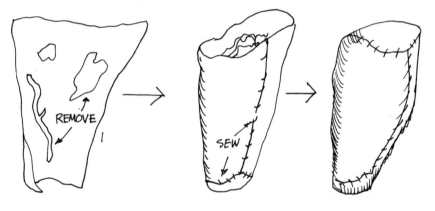

Stuffing a goose neck.

MEATS

BEEF

One of the meats we eat most frequently, as children and adults, is hamburger. Nothing can compete with an American broiled hamburger in a toasted bun, with a fresh slice of onion and some ketchup. But here is a recipe for hamburger that is a mixture of what I have learned in the United States about hamburgers and the spices I really like.

SHAHBURGER

WHAT DO YOU NEED?

1½ pounds ground beef round
Salt and pepper
Juice of one lemon
1½ teaspoons ground cumin
3 *pita* breads (little Eastern flat breads)
6 slices sweet onion
Fresh parsley
Sliced tomatoes

In a bowl, combine your chopped meat with salt, pepper, lemon juice, and cumin. Mix well. Make six hamburger patties. Broil them under the broiler the way you like them. When they are done to taste, cut each *pita* in half crosswise, and put the halves under the broiler till they are warm. Open each half up, and slide in a hamburger. Add the slice of onion, surround your hamburger with some parsley and one or two slices of tomato, and you have a "shahburger." Try this on your friends; it is really something new.

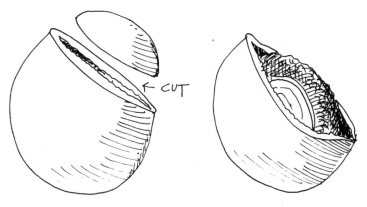

And you have a shahburger.

MEAT LOAF

Decent meat loaf is not only good hot; but, if you have any left and refrigerate it, it is delicious cold and sliced very thin, for lunch with a salad or in a sandwich.

WHAT DO YOU NEED?

½ **pound chopped beef**
½ **pound chopped veal**
½ **pound chopped pork**
1 egg
1 slice white bread, dipped in water
Salt and pepper
3 shallots, peeled and chopped
2 tablespoons chopped fresh parsley
3 hard-boiled eggs
12 green olives stuffed with pimento
2 cloves garlic, peeled and slivered
2 slices bacon
3 cups bouillon

In a bowl, put all the chopped meats together, add an egg, and mix well. Squeeze the slice of bread so that all the water is out, and add the bread to the meat. Again mix well. Add some salt, some pepper, the chopped shallots and parsley. Taste the mixture to see if it is spicy enough. Form a loaf of the meat, and open the center. (See illustration.) In the center, place in a row the

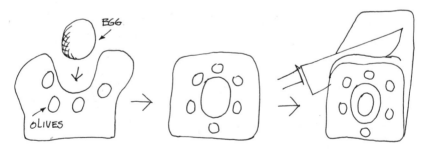

In the center place the hard-boiled eggs.

hard-boiled eggs. Surround the eggs with stuffed green olives. Close, covering the eggs with the meat. Cut the garlic in slivers and push them into different places in the meat loaf.

In a shallow roasting pan, put a slice of bacon. On top of the bacon, place your meat loaf. On top of the meat loaf, place the other slice of bacon. Pour in one cup of bouillon. Preheat your oven at 350° and cook the meat loaf for an hour, basting it often. As the water evaporates, add another cup of bouillon.

When you slice the loaf, in the center of each slice there will be a slice of hard-boiled egg surrounded by the green olives (see illustration). Scrape the pan, add another cup of bouillon, let it boil, and pour the sauce in a bowl; serve it with the meat loaf. What remains can be refrigerated and served cold, with mustard.

ROLLED BEEF WITH BACON

This is a quick dish that is very good on a hot summer night. I serve it with French fried potatoes or a nice salad.

WHAT DO YOU NEED?

4 very thin slices beef round
2 cloves garlic, cut in slivers
Salt and pepper
4 tablespoons chopped fresh parsley
4 tablespoons butter, very cold
4 slices bacon
Toothpicks

Cut each slice of beef in three equal parts. In the center of each piece of beef, put a small piece of garlic, some salt, some pepper, a little parsley, and a teaspoon of butter. Roll the beef very tight. Surround it with half a slice of bacon. The whole thing should be held together with a toothpick. When all the pieces of meat are ready, light your broiler. Broil the beef rolls for 5 minutes on each side. Serve piping hot, with French fried potatoes.

STEAK

Everybody in the U.S. can cook steak. The American people are the masters of this art. But here are a couple of tips to use when you have a steak that is not the best cut or the most tender: One, you can use meat tenderizer. I usually use a meat tenderizer that has no spice, as I like to add my own spice. You just follow the directions. Two, you can cut your steak in small slices and sauté quickly—these bits become excellent-tasting steak.

Once your steak is cooked the way you like it, one nice way of serving it is with tarragon butter. I take four tablespoons butter, one tablespoon dried tarragon, half a clove garlic (chopped), salt, and pepper. I mix all the ingredients together and divide them into small balls and cool the balls for an hour in the freezer. As I am about to serve my steak, I put on each steak a little ball of tarragon butter and serve the steak surrounded by parsley and a slice of lemon. This treatment really helps a cheaper cut of steak.

STEAK AU POIVRE

Steak au poivre is a very French way of eating steak. It is very good if you are not afraid of a burning tongue and are prepared for a fight to reach for the water pitcher.

WHAT DO YOU NEED?

2–2½ pounds beef steak, ¾ inch thick
2 tablespoons crushed black peppercorns
2 tablespoons butter
2 tablespoons oil
Sprigs of fresh parsley

For the sauce:

1 tablespoon butter
2 tablespoons minced shallots or scallions
½ cup bouillon

⅓ cup cognac
Tarragon and garlic butter (see page 168)
Parsley sprigs

Dry the steaks on a paper towel. Rub and press the peppercorns into both sides of the meat using the palm of your hand. Let the meat stand for half an hour, so that the flavor of the peppercorns gets into the steak. Each steak should not be entirely covered with peppercorns; in that case it would be so hot that one could not taste the meat.

In a heavy skillet, melt two tablespoons butter with the oil; when they bubble, cook your steaks the way you like it—rare, medium-rare, or well done. Remove the steaks, and put them on a hot platter.

Add a third tablespoon of butter to the pan. Sauté your shallots or scallions. Pour in the cognac and bouillon; boil rapidly for a minute or two, so that the alcohol of the cognac evaporates.

At the last minute, add a piece of butter mixed with tarragon and garlic (as you have done before for a regular steak, see page 168). Pour this sauce over the steak. Surround the meat with fresh parsley and serve immediately.

In France, this steak is often served with fried potatoes (see page 125) or with roasted new potatoes.

POT ROAST

My Colombian housekeeper, Lucy, makes this dish; she prepares it the night before, and cooks it the next day. I also managed to sneak in and find out how she does this one; but it is her domain, and when I buy pot roast she is the one to cook it. I would humbly make it; but my children will only eat pot roast if Lucy cooks it. But now I have the recipe, and I will share it with everybody.

WHAT DO YOU NEED?

2 large onions, peeled and sliced
3 carrots, scraped and sliced
1 celery stalk, cut in small pieces
4 cloves garlic, peeled and chopped, plus 2 whole cloves garlic
1 teaspoon salt
1 teaspoon pepper
½ teaspoon dried thyme
½ teaspoon ground cumin
2 tablespoons lemon juice
5 tablespoons oil
½ cup white wine
6 pounds beef brisket
3 slices bacon
1 onion peeled and stuck with 3 cloves
1 or 2 cups canned beef consommé
Chopped parsley

Combine the sliced onions, carrots, celery, chopped garlic, seasonings, lemon juice, oil, and wine in a large, deep bowl and put the meat in this marinade. Let the beef stand overnight, turning it over once or twice.

The next morning, in a heavy skillet, sauté two or three slices of bacon cut in little pieces. Remove the meat from the marinade. Make five or six holes with a knife in the meat. Cut the whole garlic cloves in thin slivers, and push the slivers into the meat. When the bacon fat has melted, sauté the meat in the bacon fat. Brown it on all sides. Then add the onions from the marinade plus one onion stuck with three cloves. Add all the wine from the marinade and the sliced carrots and celery. Bring to a boil. Cook, covered, on a very low flame. An hour later, add a cup or two of canned beef consommé; cook for another hour. The meat should be done when pierced easily with a fork. Taste the sauce to see if it is salty enough and has enough pepper.

Just before serving, remove the meat from the pot. Slice it and put the slices back in the sauce. Reheat without boiling. With two spatulas, remove the sliced meat, put it on a platter. Pour some sauce over the meat; surround it with chopped parsley, and serve it with rice or fresh noodles, and the rest of the sauce in a bowl. This meat is also fabulous served cold, in jelly.

BEEF IN JELLY, LUCY'S RECIPE

WHAT DO YOU NEED?

6 pounds beef brisket, pot roasted
3 eggs, hard-boiled
Black olives
Fresh parsley or tarragon
Green stuffed olives
4 cups beef jelly

Cook the meat as above (begin on page 169). Remove the meat from the sauce, and let it cool; then refrigerate it overnight. When the meat is cold, slice it thin. This can be done easily.

Prepare your beef jelly:

WHAT DO YOU NEED?

3 envelopes Knox gelatin
3 tablespoons cold water
4 cups hot beef bouillon
1 cup of the sauce in which the pot roast has been cooked,
  strained
2 tablespoons brandy

In a pot, combine the Knox gelatin and cold water. When the gelatin has softened, add quickly the hot bouillon. Mix well. Bring back to a boil. Add the strained sauce of the meat, plus a tablespoon or two of brandy. Cool. In a big mold, pour a thin layer of this beef jelly and refrigerate it.

Meanwhile, hard-boil three eggs. Cool, and peel. Slice thin. The hard-boiled eggs are to decorate the top of your mold. When the gelatin in the mold is set, make a design with the hard-boiled eggs, some black olives, parsley or fresh tarragon, green olives stuffed with pimento. Cover with another thin layer of gelatin and refrigerate. When set, cover the ingredients in the mold with one layer of meat thinly sliced. Pour some gelatin on it, add a couple of thinly sliced green olives. Refrigerate, then make another layer, and continue till you have used all the meat. When all the meat is used, pour in the rest of the gelatin. Refrigerate for 24 hours.

To serve, dip the mold for a second in boiling water, being very careful not to drip any water on the gelatin. Put a plate on top of the mold, reverse, and soon the jelly will fall onto the plate. It will look beautiful. You can decorate the jelly with more hard-boiled egg slices and pieces of parsley, or hard-boiled eggs and black olives, or hard-boiled eggs and sliced radishes. Slice the beef in jelly in wedges very thinly, as if you were slicing a cake, and serve with a nice tomato salad, or a nice green salad.

FONDUE BOURGUIGNONNE

This dish is fun to prepare, for it requires no cooking; and it is fun to eat, because everyone eats from the same pot. What you need is a fondue pot (see illustration). *Fondu* means "melted" in French; and a fondue dish comes with a Sterno or alcohol burner to keep it hot and forks with long handles to hold the food—so you won't burn yourself when you want to retrieve your bread or your meat from the cooking pot.

Fondue bourguignonne is made with beef, deep-fried in oil and eaten smothered with any sauce you like. It is good served with French or Italian bread and a big green salad.

WHAT DO YOU NEED?

3 pounds beef round, cut in bite-size pieces
Watercress

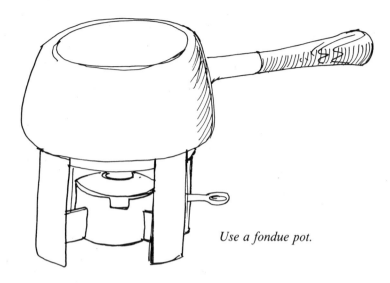

Use a fondue pot.

Small bowl *aioli* (recipe on page 95)
Small bowl coarse salt
Small bowl freshly ground pepper
Small bowl grated horseradish
2 onions, chopped
Dijon mustard
1 cup vegetable oil
Fresh Italian or French bread

Cut the meat in small pieces, removing any fat or gristle. Arrange the meat on a serving platter and decorate with watercress.

Prepare the *aioli*, following the recipe on page 95.

Horseradish is a very large white radish that is very hot; you can buy it, grated and prepared with vinegar, in a bottle in the refrigerator case in the market. Fill the bowls with salt, pepper, horseradish, onion, and mustard. Put the meat on the table and surround it with these bowls.

Heat the oil on the kitchen stove; when it is very hot, pour it into the fondue pot on top of the burner. Each guest spears a piece of meat on his fork, sticks it in the hot oil, and fries it as long as necessary to cook it the way the person likes it—rare, medium, or well done. Then the diner dips the meat in one of the sauces or seasonings, trying each one in turn until he or she finds the combination that pleases.

Be careful! Don't splash or drip hot oil on each other; and don't fight to be first, or you may burn yourself. Sometimes, when the meat is nearly gone, I like to fry a piece of my bread in the oil. The oil, by that time, has a very good taste from the juice of the meat.

POTÉE

This is one of my favorite dishes. A *potée* is chicken and beef and vegetables, cooked in a stew and served with different sauces. It is a peasant dish, but it is a spectacular dish if well done.

WHAT DO YOU NEED?

2 pounds short ribs of beef
Chicken giblets
3 or 4 marrow bones
4 quarts water
1 onion stuck with 3 cloves
1 smoked pork shoulder or butt (picnic ham), 1½ to 2 pounds
¼ pound bacon slab, in one piece
1 tablespoon salt
5 or 6 peppercorns
3 or 4 stalks parsley, plus extra for garnish
1 broiling chicken, stuffed (see page 152)
4 cabbage leaves
5 or 6 carrots
5 or 6 turnips
4 or 5 potatoes

2 or 3 leeks
Toothpicks

In a big heavy pot, put your short ribs of beef, the chicken giblets, and the marrow bones. Cover with water. When the water starts boiling, lower the heat and skim the top of the soup. Add the onion stuck with cloves. Add the ham and the bacon. Let the soup cook for an hour. Add a tablespoon of salt, five or six peppercorns, and three or four stalks of parsley.

When the beef is half done, add the chicken, prepared as you prepared for a stuffed roast chicken. Save half a cup of the stuffing for the cabbage leaves.

While the meat and the chicken are cooking, heat a big pot half full of water; when the water boils, plunge your head of cabbage in, top down, for a few minutes. Drain. Remove the first four outer leaves. Cut them in two down the center and cut off the center stems. In the middle of each half leaf, put a tablespoon of stuffing (saved from the chicken). Roll the cabbage leaves, and hold each together with a toothpick. Add stuffed leaves to the soup.

Scrape the carrots, peel the turnips, and peel and quarter the potatoes. Peel and clean the leeks (see page 98). Add these vegetables to the soup.

When the potatoes are done, and the carrots are done, your *potée* is ready. Remove the ham and slice it. Carefully remove the chicken, and put it in the center of a big platter. Surround the chicken with the short ribs of beef. In turn, surround the short ribs of beef with your sliced ham. Put some parsley sprigs around the plate. On another dish, arrange the vegetables: the stuffed cabbage, the carrots, the turnips, the potatoes, and the leeks. Pour the soup into a tureen.

You serve this meal by serving the meat and the vegetables and the soup together, which means in front of each person there should be a plate for the meat and the vegetables, and a soup bowl for the soup. Serve the *potée* with sliced hot Italian or French bread, and with *aioli* (recipe on page 95). This sauce is delicious with the *potée*. In another bowl, you make another mayonnaise (recipe on page 79), but to this one you add a tablespoon of mustard and some capers. You can also have a bowl of prepared horseradish. This is really a spectacular dish, and the soup will be very tasty and the meat and vegetables will be excellent.

LEG OF LAMB

Leg of lamb is another traditional French dish that is served for Sunday lunch. It is very easy to cook a leg of lamb. The French eat their leg of lamb medium rare—never overcooked. Buy a leg of lamb, and remove the thin hard skin with the point of a knife. Peel three or four cloves of garlic and cut them in slivers. Make some holes with a knife all over the leg of lamb, and push the garlic slivers in the holes. Rub the leg of lamb with salt and pepper, and place it in a shallow baking dish. Spread three or four tablespoons of butter on top of the leg of lamb. Add ½ cup bouillon to the pan.

Preheat your oven to 375°. When it is hot, place your leg of lamb in the oven and cook it for an hour, basting it once or twice. Use a meat thermometer stuck in the meatiest part to tell you when the lamb is done the way you like it.

When the lamb is done, remove it and put it on a platter. Surround it with watercress. Scrape the bottom part of the pan. Add another ½ cup bouillon. Boil the sauce down, correct the seasoning, and serve it in a separate bowl.

With a leg of lamb very often I serve canned lima beans or canned white beans called flageolets. You can find them where Spanish food is sold in supermarkets. They are white beans that look like lima beans. Drain the can, rinse the beans under cold water, drain them. In a heavy pot melt three tablespoons of butter. When the butter is melted, add the beans. Sauté to heat them, and add salt and pepper to taste. Sprinkle with parsley. Sometimes, to make the beans even better, I add ½ cup heavy cream. But, remember, don't let the heavy cream boil.

BRAISED SHOULDER OF LAMB WITH LENTILS

The following recipe was given to me by my friend Edith Ferber, an excellent cook. She lived in an old house in Vermont; when our tribe (six people) would descend upon her, this is what she would serve us after a long walk in the snow or a ride on the toboggan.

WHAT DO YOU NEED?

1 shoulder of lamb, boned and tied
4 cloves garlic
Salt and pepper
½ teaspoon each dried thyme and marjoram
2 cups lentils
1 onion, stuck with several cloves
1 bay leaf
5 cups water
1 cup Madeira or Port wine
1 teaspoon dry mustard
6 slices bacon

Have the butcher bone and tie the lamb for you. Cut the garlic in slivers; pierce the meat with a knife (in a number of places) and insert the garlic slivers. Rub the meat with salt and pepper, and sprinkle it with the thyme and marjoram. Put the lamb on a rack in a roasting pan and roast for one hour at 375°.

Meanwhile, wash the lentils; put the lentils, onion, and bay leaf in a heavy pot that can go in the oven, and add the water. Cover and bring to a boil on top of the stove; lower heat and simmer for 30 minutes.

When lamb is ready, transfer to pot with lentils; add the wine and the mustard, and cover the pot. Lower oven heat to 325° and bake lamb and lentils for 1 hour more.

Fry the bacon crisp; and, when you are ready to serve, crumble it over the lentils.

VEAL SCALOPPINE WITH MARINATED MUSHROOMS

Scaloppine are very thin slices of veal cut either from the loin or the leg of the calf. They are expensive; and if you replace the veal scaloppine with thin veal chops, the preparation and cooking are the same.

WHAT DO YOU NEED?

3 tablespoons butter
6 scaloppine or 6 thin veal chops
Flour
Juice of ½ lemon
4-ounce jar marinated mushrooms
1 tablespoon dried tarragon
Salt and pepper
Chopped parsley

In a heavy skillet, melt the butter. Sprinkle the scaloppine with flour. When the butter is bubbling, sauté your veal. The scaloppine should cook very fast, in 2 or 3 minutes on each side. When the scaloppine are done, add the lemon juice and the marinated mushrooms, with the juice in which they come. Add the tablespoon of tarragon, sprinkle with salt and pepper. Taste the juice of the meat to see if the seasoning is correct; if not, add salt or pepper. Transfer the scaloppine onto a platter. Pour over them the mushrooms and all the juice in which they have cooked. Sprinkle with some chopped parsley, and serve with rice (see page 128).

BREADED PORK CHOPS

WHAT DO YOU NEED?

6 lean pork chops
⅓ cup olive oil
Juice of 1 lemon
Salt and pepper
1 egg mixed with 1 tablespoon water
¼ cup fine bread crumbs
⅓ cup Parmesan cheese
2 tablespoons butter and olive oil
Chopped fresh parsley
½ cup bouillon (made with a cube)

Marinate the pork chops in a mixture of the olive oil, lemon juice, and salt and pepper for about two hours. Drain the chops and pat them dry with a paper towel. Then beat the egg with the water. Coat each pork chop on both sides with the egg, then dip them in the bread crumbs mixed with the Parmesan cheese. In a heavy skillet, melt the butter and the olive oil. When the butter bubbles, add the pork chops. Brown them on each side. Cover the skillet and put the chops in an oven at 325° for about 25–30 minutes. They are done when they feel tender when you test them with a fork.

Remove the chops from the skillet, put them on a platter, sprinkle with some chopped parsley. Add ½ cup hot bouillon to the pan and scrape; boil this sauce down, pour it in a bowl, and serve with the pork chops. Also nice to serve with the pork chops are applesauce and rice.

BREADED PORK CHOPS
WITH OLIVES

Another way to cook the chops is to use the same method, but not to bake the pork chops; instead, continue cooking them slowly in the heavy skillet on top of the stove. You should add another tablespoon of butter, and pour in at the last minute about a dozen pitted green olives. When the chops are tender, remove them from the pan, sprinkle with chopped parsley, and put a slice of lemon on each. Then add ¼ cup of bouillon and scrape the bottom of the frying pan. Boil it down, correct the seasoning, and pour the sauce along with the olives over the meat. This way also makes pork chops delicious.

CHOUCROUTE GARNIE

Choucroute, which is made with sauerkraut, is the national dish of Alsace—a province of France that is near the German border. If Americans knew about *choucroute*, it would become another national dish; because nearly everyone eats sauerkraut in the United States, and this dish is great!

WHAT DO YOU NEED?

3 pounds sauerkraut
¼ pound slab bacon, diced
4 garlic cloves, peeled and quartered
10 peppercorns
1½ cups white wine
1 medium ham butt
6 smoked pork chops
6–12 sausages—any kind you like: kielbasa, bratwurst, link pork sausage, weisswurst, frankfurters, etc.
Salt
6 small potatoes, peeled
Dijon mustard
Pickles

Wash the sauerkraut under running water and drain well. In a heavy saucepan, sauté the diced bacon until nearly crisp; add the garlic and cook for a minute or two. Stir in the sauerkraut, peppercorns, and wine. Cover the pot and simmer for one hour.

In another pot, cover the ham butt with water and simmer for one hour or until tender when pierced by a fork.

After one hour, add the pork chops and kielbasa, if you are using it, to the sauerkraut (cut sausages in serving pieces), and cook for one more hour. Meanwhile, boil the potatoes in salted water until tender. After 40 minutes of the second hour, add the other types of sausages to the *choucroute*.

To serve: Slice the ham. Arrange the sauerkraut on a platter with all the meats on top; surround with boiled potatoes. Serve with hot Dijon mustard and *cornichons*—small cucumber pickles.

FISH AND SHELLFISH

In France, we eat fish very often, especially on Friday, when it is plentiful. You can broil fish, bake it, or fry it. To select fish, you have to look for those with bright, clear, bulging eyes and gills that look and smell clean. The scales of the fish must be shiny and lie close to the skin; and, in general, the fish should shine.

Fish is very perishable. When you buy fish, always plan to cook it that day. If you must keep it, clean it first (remove the scales and innards) and then wrap the fish tightly in a plastic bag or foil, and keep refrigerated for one day. Most fish are bought already cleaned in the fish market. When you want to poach fish, you should ask the fish man to give you a head or two, to make the court bouillon. Court bouillon is the stock one makes with fish heads and fish tails before one poaches a fish.

Quite a number of fish resemble each other; therefore, the cooking methods and recipes can very often be interchanged. Never overcook fish. Cook fish only until it flakes easily with a fork. Fat fish are better if they are baked or broiled. Lean fish can be broiled or baked if they are frequently basted with a sauce. Most fish can be fried.

TROUT MIGNETTE

The trout in this recipe can be replaced by perch, or flounder, or sole.

WHAT DO YOU NEED?

6 small trout
1 cup milk
2 cups flour
¾ stick butter (6 tablespoons)
4 tablespoons vegetable oil
1 teaspoon lemon juice
1 lemon, sliced very thin
¼ cup chopped fresh parsley

Wash the trout very carefully under running water. Be sure that no scales are left. Dry the fish well with paper towels. Make two crosswise slashes two inches apart in the skin on each side of the fish. Dip the trout in the milk, then in the flour, then grab each fish by the tail and shake it well so that all the excess flour will fall off. In a large skillet, melt 4 tablespoons of the butter with the oil until they are very hot. Then brown the trout on both sides. The whole cooking of the trout should take no more than 12–15 minutes. Remove the trout carefully with a spatula. Pour out the fat that is in the frying pan; melt two tablespoons butter in another pan and cook the butter until it is golden brown. Add about one teaspoon of lemon juice, and pour the butter and the lemon juice over the trout. Surround the trout with slices of lemon and sprinkle it with parsley.

POACHED STRIPED BASS

WHAT DO YOU NEED?

6 cups water
2 cups dry white wine
1 fish head

1 onion
6 peppercorns
1 clove garlic
1 teaspoon dried thyme
1 teaspoon dried tarragon
1 striped bass, about 4–5 pounds
Pepper
Salt to taste
1 carrot, scraped and sliced

In a heavy saucepan, combine the water and the wine. Wash the fish head, and add it to the water. Put in one whole onion, the peppercorns, garlic and herbs, salt to taste, and the carrot; bring to a boil. This is called a court bouillon. Boil the court bouillon for about 10–15 minutes. Taste it to see if the seasoning is correct. While the broth is cooking, prepare the striped bass. Wash it under running water. Dry it with a paper towel. Rub it with salt and pepper, inside and out. Take a big piece of heavy aluminum foil, and wrap your fish in it, tightly. Put the fish in the court bouillon and cook it for 40 minutes. Open the foil, test the fish with a fork; it should flake easily. If the fish is cooked, remove it to a hot platter.

You can serve this poached striped bass with different sauces. A good sauce is a béchamel made with the court bouillon (use the recipe on pages 51–52). Or, you could make a hollandaise sauce (see pages 113–114) and add some capers and lemon juice to it. My favorite sauce with poached fish is this egg and lemon sauce:

EGG AND LEMON SAUCE

WHAT DO YOU NEED?

2 egg yolks
1 cup poaching liquid
2 tablespoons fresh lemon juice
Salt and pepper to taste

Beat the egg yolks until they are a very pale lemon color. Slowly, while beating, add one cup of the hot liquid in which your fish has poached. Cook over hot water until the sauce is slightly thickened, stirring it constantly. If you are stirring it with a wooden spoon, when the wooden spoon is coated with the sauce, the sauce is done. Add two tablespoons of fresh lemon juice, salt, and fresh ground pepper. Serve at once, with the poached striped bass.

BROILED STUFFED BLUEFISH

WHAT DO YOU NEED?

1 big bluefish (about 3 pounds)
4 tablespoons butter, plus extra butter
2 shallots, peeled and chopped
4 mushrooms, washed and chopped
1 cup bread crumbs
4 or 5 anchovy filets, chopped
2 tablespoons capers
2 tablespoons grated Parmesan cheese
Salt (optional)
A pinch of pepper
2 tablespoons chopped fresh parsley, plus sprigs for
  garnish
Toothpicks
Oil
Sliced lemon

Wash your fish carefully, and pat it dry with paper towels. Meanwhile, melt the butter. Sauté the shallots and mushrooms in the butter. When the shallots are transparent, they are done. In a bowl, combine the bread crumbs, chopped anchovies, capers, Parmesan cheese; and add the butter with the shallots and mushrooms. Mix well. Correct the seasoning. Do not add salt until you taste the stuffing. Add a pinch of pepper and the chopped parsley. If the stuffing is too dry, melt another two tablespoons butter and add to the stuffing. Make two slashes on each side of the fish. Fill the cavity of the fish with the stuffing. Close the opening with toothpicks. Set the fish on a shallow pan (oiled) and brush your fish with melted butter. Put it underneath the broiler. Cook 8–10 minutes on one side; then turn. Brush the fish again with butter and broil 5–6 minutes. Test your fish with a fork. If it flakes, the fish is done. Remove the fish. Set it on a platter. Remove the toothpicks and surround the fish with fresh parsley and sliced lemon.

The toothpicks may burn in the broiler. Don't worry about this, because you will remove them when the fish is done. Be sure not to put the fish too close to the flame, as the skin of the fish will burn, but the fish will not cook.

FILET OF SOLE WITH CREAMED SPINACH

WHAT DO YOU NEED?

Waxed paper
2 pounds spinach
6 shallots, peeled and chopped
6 filets of sole
Salt and pepper
1 cup white wine
2 tablespoons butter, plus extra butter
½ cup heavy cream
1 lemon, sliced

Wash the spinach and cook with the shallots, following the directions on page 110. Drain, press out all the water, and chop the spinach very fine; set aside.

Dry the filets of sole; salt and pepper them. Fold each one in half crosswise and place them in a buttered baking dish; pour the wine over the fish. Cover the dish with buttered waxed paper and bake the fish in a 325° oven for 15 minutes. Using two spatulas, carefully remove the fish filets from the pan (they break easily) and place them on a serving dish; keep them warm (I often do this by putting the dish back in the oven with the heat turned off and the door open a little).

Strain the juice left in the baking dish into a frying pan, add the heavy cream, and simmer until the mixture is reduced by half. Remove from the heat and stir in two tablespoons butter cut into little pieces. Add the spinach to this sauce, taste it, and add salt and pepper if it needs it.

Spread the creamed spinach on a serving dish; arrange the fish on top; brush the fish with melted butter; and decorate with lemon slices.

FRESH CODFISH BALLS

In France, as in the United States, codfish is plentiful; it can be bought fresh or dry and salted. When I was young, my mother always fixed codfish on Fridays in the winter—I hated Friday! Years later, while fishing on a pier on Cape Cod, my son Thomas befriended an old fisherman. One night, the old man invited Thomas to share his dinner and served him fresh codfish balls. Thomas, who never ate fish at home, came back raving about these codfish balls. I asked the old man for his recipe. Here it is, slightly changed:

WHAT DO YOU NEED?

**2½ cups water
1 onion, peeled, plus 2 tablespoons chopped onion
1 teaspoon salt
5 peppercorns
1 bay leaf
1 pound fresh codfish
1 stick butter (8 tablespoons)**

6 tablespoons flour
2 tablespoons chopped mushrooms
2 tablespoons chopped parsley
1 teaspoon paprika
2 tablespoons heavy cream
2 eggs
1 cup bread crumbs
Oil
Lettuce
Lemon sauce (page 183)

Boil the water with the whole onion, salt, peppercorns, and bay leaf for a few minutes. Add the fish and simmer for 6 minutes, until the fish flakes when you prick it with a fork. Drain the fish, and reserve the fish bouillon.

With ¾ stick butter (six tablespoons) and the flour, make a *roux,* following the directions on page 29; stir in 1 cup hot fish bouillon instead of milk to make a sauce. Cook the sauce, stirring, for about 10 minutes—it should be quite thick. Stir the fish into the sauce; it will break into tiny pieces as you stir.

In a small frying pan, sauté the chopped mushrooms and chopped onion in the remaining ¼ stick butter (two tablespoons); add the chopped parsley and the paprika and stir the whole mixture into the fish and sauce. Add the heavy cream, and put the mixture in the refrigerator for 20 minutes. Meanwhile, separate the eggs. Beat the whites stiff; add the yolks to the cooled sauce; then fold in the whites. Taste the mixture; see if it needs salt or pepper.

Form the fish mixture into balls. I do this by spooning up a tablespoonful at a time and rolling it in my hands. Roll each ball in bread crumbs. In your deep-fat fryer, heat the oil to 385°, and fry the balls for 5 minutes or until they are golden-brown. Drain the codfish balls on paper towels; serve hot on a bed of lettuce, with lemon sauce on the side (recipe on page 183).

SHRIMPS WITH GARLIC

This is a lovely shrimp dish that my friend the sculptor Gonzalo Fonseca always makes for me. It is a Spanish dish, and he allowed me to divulge the recipe.

WHAT DO YOU NEED?

1½ pounds small raw shrimps
¾ cup olive oil
3 cloves garlic
1 tablespoon chopped parsley
½ teaspoon salt

Shell and devein the raw shrimps, leaving the tails intact, as you have learned to do in Chapter 2 (see pages 60–61). In a bowl, mix the olive oil with the garlic, the parsley, and the salt. Stir in the shrimps, and let them marinate in the garlic and olive oil for about an hour. Then remove the shrimps and put them in a small casserole that will go into the oven. Pour the oil with the garlic over the shrimps, and bake them in a very hot oven, 375°, for 5–7 minutes, or until the shrimps turn pink. Remove the garlic cloves and serve the shrimps hot, leaving them in the casserole. Serve them with rice.

INDEX

Lettuce, 130–132
    Boston, 131–132
    iceberg, 130–131
Lima bean salad, 81–82, 142
Lime soufflé, 25–26
Liver pâté, 69, 72–73
Lobster bisque, 100–101
Lucy's recipe for beef in jelly, 171–172

Marrow balls, beef soup with, 92–93
Mayonnaise:
    garlic *(aioli)*, 94–95, 172–174
    making, 79–80
    tomato, hard-boiled eggs stuffed with, 80–81
Meat loaf, 166–167
Meats, 164–181
    beef, 164–176
    lamb, 176–178
    pork chops, 179–181
    sauce, for pasta, 84
    veal, 178
Melon and prosciutto, 82
Mousse, 20–24
    chocolate, 22–24
    coffee, 20–21
    cranberry, 21
    ham, 64–66
    rhubarb, 21–22
Mushrooms, 122–124
    and cheese, crêpes filled with, 58–59
    cream soup, 99
    marinated, veal scaloppine with, 178
    in *quiche Lorraine*, 47
    sautéed, with cream, 123–124
    stuffed, 76–77
Mustard vinaigrette, escarole with, 138–139

Oeufs en gelée (eggs in aspic), 63–64
Olives, breaded pork chops with, 179–180

Onion:
    quiche *(quiche aux oignons)*, 48–49
    soup, with cheese *(soupe à l'oignon au gratin)*, 106–107

Parsley and butter, boiled cauliflower with, 115
Parsnips, endive with, 122
Pasta, 83–85
    fettucine *alla carbonara*, 84–85
    meat sauce for, 84
    tomato sauce for, 84
Pâte à choux (puff pastry), 34–37
    as an appetizer, 56–57
    chicken soup with, 89
    dough for, 34–36
    profiteroles, 36–37
Pâtés, 66–73
    en croûte, 70–72
    pork liver, 72–73
Pears, poached, 18–19
Pea soup, 103
Pepper flakes and butter, chicken rolled with, 158
Pies, 10–18
    apple tarte, 14–15
    apricot, 13–14
    crème anglaise in, 15–18
    crust for, 12–13
    dough for, 11–12
    strawberry tarte, 16–18
Pork chops, 179–181
    breaded, 179
    breaded, with olives, 179–180
    choucroute garnie, 180–181
Pork liver pâté, 72–73
Pot roast, 169–171
Potato(es), 124–127
    French fried, 125
    gratin dauphinois, 126–127
    and leek soup, 97–98
    mashed, 126
    new, 124
    salad, 146–147